I0008614

THE CEO'S MANUAL ON CYBER SECURITY

JAMES SCOTT

The CEO's Manual on Cyber Security

A New Renaissance Corporation publication
First Edition

ISBN-13: 978-0-9892535-9-8
ISBN-10: 0989253597

Publisher:
New Renaissance Corporation
73 Old Dublin Pike, Suite 10 # 142
Doylestown, PA 18901

www.newrenaissancecorporation.com

ABOUT THE AUTHOR

James Scott is a consultant, lecturer and "Six Time Best Selling Author" on the topics of IPO facilitation, corporate structuring, Private Placement Memorandum authoring and Mergers and Acquisitions strategies. Mr. Scott has authored multiple books such as 'The Book on Mergers and Acquisitions', 'Taking Your Company Public', 'The Book on PPMs: Regulation D 504 Edition', 'The Book on PPMs: Regulation D 505 Edition', 'The Book on PPMs: Regulation D 506 Edition', 'The CEO Manual 4 Kids' as well as several templates that make the process of completing complicated S1 and PPM docs as easy as 'point and click' for entrepreneurs and corporate CEOs. Mr. Scott is a member of several economic think tanks that study diverse aspects of legislation concepts that affect corporations worldwide such as: Aspen Institute, Chatham House: Royal Institute of International Affairs, The American Enterprise Institute, Economic Research Council, American Institute for Economic Research, The Manhattan Institute and The Hudson Institute among others.

To contact James Scott visit the 'Contact Us' page at the New Renaissance Corporation publishing website: www.newrenaissancecorporation.com

| CONTENTS

PREFACE

THE IMPORTANCE OF PROACTIVE MEASURES ON CYBERSPACE SECURITY

Since 2002, there has been an enormous increase in the number of known server vulnerabilities, leaving the traditional defensive solutions far behind.

If you have been booked into a city or county jail in Washington state between September 2011 and December 2012, you may be at risk of having your Social Security number and associated data exposed. The data exposed may include your full name and driver's license number.

Because of the vulnerability in Adobe's ColdFusion app server, a cyber attacker could enter servers operated by the Washington State Court System. They have exposed data belonging to over one million members of the US public. The exposure includes 160,000 Social Security numbers.

Such **web attacks** are nothing new; today, attackers have improved on the sophistication used and the nature of the crime has changed. For example, web attacks between 2008 and 2010 caused 53 Seattle based enterprises to face damages worth $3 million. Most such attacks are because of complacency and not remaining alert to the threat. Vulnerable Wi-Fi networks, malicious e-mails and harmful websites only add to the seriousness of the problem.

For countering such web attacks, enterprises must necessarily improve their employee education; install anti-virus and anti-malware protection on both their mobile and their non-mobile devices.

Employee education is all the more important, as crooks find it easier to exploit human nature to gain access to information. Non-technical intrusions involving and relying heavily on human interaction, otherwise known as **social engineering**, often involves inducing people to break security procedures normally used.

The most common form of social engineering mimics the names of well-known companies and sends fake-emails. Receiving a threat mail from the Fed to take fake security measures is well known. The misleading alert induces the user to divulge authentic login information to a website, often the victim's bank account. Pop-up messages often confuse victims by tricking them into believing they are a part of the computer's security system, when they are actually generated from online advertisements, social networking sites and search engine results.

Being proactive in terms of employee education and developing a framework for security management in defining a set of security goals against social engineering can assist enterprises in staying one step ahead. It is also necessary for the enterprises to implement defenses against social engineering within their security policy.

Enterprises offering web services must take proactive measures to prevent their servers from being made targets of **denial of service** (DOS) to authentic clients. The denial of service attack usually takes the form of locking out the authentic users through a deluge of activity, clogging the access network. Business and revenue remain severely undermined for the duration of the attack, and enterprises are known to have had to pay the attackers to be allowed to regain control, resulting in plunging customer relationships, bottom lines, and brand reputation.

Enterprises must build up their defenses by locking down Domain Name System (DNS) servers, using enhanced DNS protection and balance their load among redundant servers spread over several datacenters.

Most denial of service, DOS or DDOS as it is commonly known, is caused by **botnets**. Botnets are a web of compromised computers, which attackers use to generate and send e-mail spam, steal identity information, capture credit card details and credentials such as usernames and passwords. Unless enterprises are proactive in warding off such attacks, botnets can cause excessive damage not only to the revenue and the business, but also to the reputation of the enterprise.

Proactive enterprises would scan their systems to detect and remove any traces of malware planted to compromise the system to botnets. Tools such as AntiBot and RUBotted are a great help in such scenarios. Other measures for insulating computers against botnets involve the use of latest software, installing anti-virus and anti-malware programs.

Cloud hacks are now a common threat as use of cloud services and cloud connected devices mushroom. To cut down on the cost of infrastructure and to enhance the overall effectiveness of the enterprise, many organizations use cloud-based services such as software as a service, platform as a service and cloud storage services. Although their own perimeters may be securely locked down, accessing and sending data across the firewall to a cloud has its own vulnerabilities.

Being the custodian of customer data, the enterprise has the moral obligation to protect confidential data from cloud hacking, with proactive measures such as customer education and use of encryption. Customers must be coaxed into using complicated passwords or use password generators such as LastPass and RoboForm. If the enterprise encrypts the data on their servers, customers must be instructed to keep their encryption keys as safe as the keys of their bank vaults.

Unless they have taken proactive measures to protect themselves, enterprises are vulnerable to the misuse of and **attacks via the Universal Serial Bus (USB)** ports existing in all devices, both portable and desk computers. Enterprises using the Microsoft Windows Operating Systems are most vulnerable to this threat, because of the AutoRun feature of the OS. This allows any executable file on the inserted USB device to be detected automatically and executed.

Attackers usually hide their malware in such auto-executable files and have them transferred to the system by USB devices operated by unsuspecting users. The malware, once inside, can replicate in the system, compromising it entirely.

Proactive measures would include having a company-wide policy using only permitted USB devices, and detecting and blocking other non-permitted USB devices.

If the enterprise serves web pages to their clients, they could face attacks from **clickjacking and cross-site scripting**, that is, unless they have taken adequate measures to prevent such attacks from affecting them in the first place. Attackers usually overlay a legitimate website with an invisible button and entice the user to click on it. This clickjacking can have serious consequences for the user, making them give up their credentials, and even making them do some things they would not do in the normal course of events.

Vulnerabilities in web applications served by an enterprise can be attacked with cross-site scripting, where the attacker can place a malicious code into the dynamic web page. When the user unsuspectingly opens the page in their browser, the malicious code enters their system and creates havoc.

Enterprises must alert and train their programmers against such attacks and regularly use scanners to detect vulnerabilities in their websites. They must insist on their clients using the latest browsers with all the securities turned on.

Proactive enterprises can help their organizations avoid **phishing attacks from trusted third parties**. These are usually messages, from purportedly trusted senders asking users to click on a provided link for updating their data. User credentials will be required to enter the data, and the phisher gathers the information. The trusted third parties that phishers normally impersonate are e-pay systems, e-auction systems and banks.

Proactive employee education serves to protect users within the enterprise against phishing and pharming. Teaching employees to detect suspicious looking e-mails and delete them helps lessen this threat. All the latest browsers have built-in protection against phishing, and the enterprise must aggressively upgrade all browsers they use.

Enterprises may face attacks not only from the outside, but also from their own employees. **Data exfiltration** may be one of the threats where malicious employees of the enterprise move data out to share with competitors for potential gains. Such removal of data may be via e-mails, printing on paper, scanning, faxing and/or using copiers. Depending on the data taken out, the damage to the enterprise may be incalculable, resulting in loss of future earnings and loss of credibility.

A proactive enterprise would use central logging to store and index insider behavior on their networks. All devices used by the enterprise would be incorporated into risk assessment and would use policies to govern their use.

With the advent of BYOD, employees are encouraged to Bring Your Own Devices to work at enterprises. This has encouraged more **attacks on mobile devices and wireless networks**. While attacks on smartphones and other mobile devices may not be a direct threat to the enterprise, the compromised device may become a threat when used as a pivot vector to attack the network of the enterprise. The attacker may have wide-open access to the enterprise network.

Proactive enterprises usually protect their wireless networks from such attacks by protecting their WLAN switches as they manage access to several points in the network. Such enterprises, although encouraging BYOD, create a process for evaluating all mobile apps that employees use. Moreover, constant use of intrusion detection systems and malware detection systems along with a firewall help to keep the enterprise up to date.

When an attack is discovered, the speed in which the enterprise is able to remove all traces of the attacker from its networks and get back in operation is crucial. This is dependent on a credible **data recovery capability** of the enterprise. This capability is usually a careful balance of Recovery Time Objective (RTO) and Recovery Point Objective (RPO), the downtime that the enterprise can bear and the amount of loss the enterprise can withstand.

Proactive enterprises typically invest in multiple off-site backup solutions and encryption of stored data. Imperatively, periodical testing of the backups should confirm they would stand up to cases of an actual attack.

Business critical applications may be vulnerable to **SSRF attacks** or Server Side Request Forgery attacks. Enterprises usually run business application infrastructures such as Enterprise Resource Planning (ERP), Customer Resource Management (CRM), and Storage Resource Management (SRM). These systems are critical to the operation of the enterprise as they hold data on sensitive issues such as finance and personnel, and are often connected to banking client workstations.

Since most business applications are purchased from vendors, proactive enterprises monitor the system with automated solutions such as ERPScan Security Scanners. They let application security experts assess the systems and have close collaborations with the vendor to close the detected vulnerabilities.

Despite using Hypertext Transport Protocol Secure (HTTPS) traffic and making sure of encrypting authentication cookies, attackers can overcome these defenses and use Compression Ratio Info-Leak Made Easy (**CRIME**) to exploit the data compression scheme to collect sensitive information.

Proactive enterprises protect their computers and networks against outsider and insider malware attacks by using anti-malware, anti-spyware and anti-virus programs. Taking it one step further, enterprises keep their browsers up to date and use proper security policies and security systems such as firewalls.

Enterprises can be compromised when using **vulnerable chrome extensions**. Although most chrome extensions are safe enough, some are not so secure. Through these non-secure extensions, an attacker can gain access to a system and execute a malicious JavaScript to do further damage.

Proactive enterprises will continuously monitor their network for virus, Trojans and malware. Through their security policy, such enterprises will allow only secure extensions to be used in the browsers they use in-house.

Some browser sessions make it convenient for the user to not have to log in repeatedly by remembering their username and password. Although this may be a convenience for the user, it is also convenient for a malicious attacker, who can then dig out the user's credentials by using the **BruteForce of PHPSESSID**. The attacker uses the session ID token issued by the server when the session starts. After hijacking the session, the attacker repeatedly requests the server with guessed usernames and passwords, forcing a denial of service to other users. After gaining an entry into the victim's account, not only can he steal information, he can also plant malware to compromise other accounts on the server.

Enterprises dealing with such servers must proactively use effective methods such as CAPTCHA[1] and assign unique login URLs to sections of users. They must also automatically place illegally accessed accounts in lockdown mode with limited capabilities.

Enterprises use CAPTCHA on their websites to differentiate a computer trying to read the page from a human. However, a **CAPTCHA re-riding** attack may be used to bypass the CAPTCHA system and send repeated requests to the server to create multiple accounts on the server. Attackers expose millions of emails this way and put them up for sale. Attackers also exploit data related to the government, intelligent agencies and the military.

Proactive enterprises thwart such CAPTCHA re-riding attacks by resetting the CAPTCHA solution within the HTTP session as soon as the verification stage completes.

A permanent network compromise may also come from a single threat with many hidden vectors. These are usually **blended threats and JavaScript**, which target the host browser with a single malicious JavaScript, while releasing further worms, Trojans and backdoors into the system. A successful attack leads the attacker to gain access to sensitive information and/or privilege escalation.

Most enterprises proactively follow RFC-5735, while not allowing sites from the internet to access internal private IP addresses. They also enable protection for Cross-site request forgery (CSRF) on all embedded devices. Blended threats and JavaScript can also be detected by establishing new heuristics.

Hypertext Markup Language (HTML) widgets embedded in websites may cause severe security concerns because of **Permanent backdooring of HTML5 client-side applications**. Although use of HTML5 improves the performance of mobile users, the local storage and caching on the client devices may become a haven for attackers. They can create and store permanent backdoors in these applications, operating unnoticed whenever the application is started. The backdoor can log keystrokes thus steal usernames and passwords, inject Trojans into the system and steal session cookies.

Proactive enterprises protect their web pages against manipulation of XSS (Cross-Site Scripting) vulnerabilities and malicious advertisements. On the client side, they use only whitelisted applications.

Security flaws in high-profile web sites may lead to **XSS attacks**. Malicious attackers have gained access to user information including credit card details and carried out expensive transactions. Using similar methods, they have also gained access to enterprise databases, causing a loss of customer faith and goodwill.

Proactive measures taken by enterprises include the use of HTTPOnly[2], enabling key security controls of the web applications and carrying out security testing regularly on the website.

Enterprises using OData or Open Data Protocol can allow their clients many facilities for handling, updating and querying information in their databases. Since the protocol used by OData does not include any security specifications, **attacks on OData** are frequent. It is the responsibility of the enterprise using OData to implement necessary security best fitting to their target scenario.

Proactive steps to mitigate the risks involved in using OData require the enterprise to implement various data validation scenarios, including using injection attacks.

Other proactive measures used by enterprises for cyber security involve:

- Use of secure configurations for all devices including network devices;

- Keeping wireless devices under control;

- Keeping application software security under control;

- Keeping administrative privileges under control;

- Maintaining an inventory of all authorized and unauthorized devices;

- Maintaining an inventory of all authorized and unauthorized software;

- Maintaining, monitoring and analyzing audit logs;

- Having a process of continuous vulnerability assessment and remediation.

Apart from all the above steps, enterprises should use good security policies implemented company-wide, combined with continuous employee education and promoting good coding practices. Following suggestions from the Code Secure Blog will also avoid threats such as clickjacking.

1

ANYONE CAN BE PWNED THROUGH CHROME EXTENSION HACKS

WHAT IS PWNING THROUGH CHROME EXTENSION HACKS?

Pwning, in hacker jargon, refers to compromising or controlling another's website, computer, application or gateway device. Some security researchers even award Pwnie Awards for cracking.

Although Google claims that its browser, Chrome, is the safest web browser on the market, one can never be too careful in matters concerning security. There are indeed several Chrome extensions with which you could lock down Chrome and make it extremely secure.

However, other extensions of Chrome are not so secure, and can be used by attackers to compromise the Chrome browser. For example, the ScratchPad Extension allows users to take notes and auto-syncs the note files with Google Docs in the ScratchPad folder. One of the features of this extension allows users to share ScratchPad folders without the need for any permission from the original user.

HOW CAN ATTACKERS USE VULNERABLE CHROME EXTENSIONS?

A malicious code hidden in one of the notes saved on the ScratchPad folder, when accessed by the victim can compromise his browser. Once the note is opened, the code proceeds to steal all contacts saved in the victim's Gmail account, since he was already logged into it. Although Google has now patched this specific vulnerability, there are several other extensions with similar or worse vulnerabilities.

With increased use of mobile devices, attacks on applications are rising. Many powerful chrome extensions are meant for the user to access cloud services through Chrome, and this is becoming the main target for attackers.

Most mobile apps require user permission for accessing the various features and capabilities. Extensions for the Chrome OS also require permissions to access features and capabilities, but the difference is, permissions are set and defined by the developer of the extension.

With independent software developers writing the Chrome OS extensions, the security mindset of the developers becomes more important to define the vulnerability/security of the software.

WHAT HAPPENS DURING AN ATTACK ON A VULNERABLE CHROME OS EXTENSION?

With increased focus on cloud-based applications and storage, malware is not downloadable from the cloud to the user's machine. The usual suspects are weeded out by the Chrome OS and users remain protected.

Therefore, instead of targeting the data on the user's hard disk, the attacker targets the applications that send and receive data between the cloud service and the Chrome browser.

Attackers target common web vulnerabilities that can compromise higher privileged applications. They use Cross Site Request Forgery and Cross Site Scripting vulnerabilities, which are the most common in such extensions. As independent developers write most extensions, writing bad code is common, and the developer may provide the extension with more permissions than is necessary.

- Once exploited, the attacker can:

- Monitor all the open tabs on the victim's browser

- Execute a malicious JavaScript on every tab

- Extract HTML Code from the web pages

- Read/Write cookies stored in the browser

- Access the local hard disk of the victim

- Manipulate the history of the victim's browser

- Take screenshots of the tabs on the browser

- Inject keyloggers/ BeEF hooks for causing further damage

HOW CAN PWNING THROUGH CHROME EXTENSION HACKS BE PREVENTED?

Awareness of which extensions provide greater security to Chrome affords the best protection from these attacks. Some of these extensions enhance the inherent security of the Chrome browser. External vigilance and continuous monitoring for malware, Trojans, and virus is essential. Some of the more secure extensions that help prevent attacks are:

- Google Alarm
- FlashBlock
- BugMeNot Lite
- AdBlock
- Secure Profile
- TrustGuard
- Credit Card Nanny
- PasswordFail
- KB SSL Enforcer
- View Thru
- Click & Clean
- Secbrowsing
- LastPass
- SiteAdvisor
- Web of Trust

REFERENCES:

1. Osborn, K,. Kotowicz, K., BlackHat USA2012, *Advanced Chrome Extension Exploitation*. Available from: <http://media.blackhat.com/bh-us-12/Briefings/Osborn/BH_US_12_Osborn_Kotowicz_Advanced_Chrome_Extension_Slides.pdf>. [2013].

2. Notebook Review, *15 Best Google Chrome Security Extensions*. Available from: <http://www.notebookreview.com/default.asp?newsID=5796&review=15+Best+Google+Chrome+Security+Extensions>. [10 August 2010].

3. Rashid, F. Y., eWeek, *Google Chrome OS Hacked Using ScratchPad Extension in Black Hat Preview*. Available from: <http://www.eweek.com/c/a/Mobile-and-Wireless/Google-Chrome-OS-Hacked-Using-ScratchPad-Extension-in-Black-Hat-Preview-343583/>. [14 July 2011].

4. Kaplan, D., CRN, *Chrome extension hack pwns everyone*. Available from: <http://www.crn.com.au/News/266119,chrome-extension-hack-pwns-everyone.aspx>. [8 Aug 2011].

2 | BOTNETS: WHAT ARE THEY? AND HOW TO PROTECT YOUR COMPANY FROM THEM

WHAT ARE BOTNETS?

Bot, a short form for robot, is an automated program which allows external sources to control a computer remotely. The user is usually not aware of the infection. When several computers are affected in this manner, they network together to form a botnet, which is under the covert control of a command-and-control server. A botmaster is usually in control of such a server.

Without the users' knowledge, their computers are hooked up to botnet, and the botmaster can then employ them for a variety of wicked purposes. Most botmasters use the bots in the botnets to accomplish up to three main goals, not particularly in the given sequence:

- Generating and sending E-mail spam;

- Stealing identity information, user credentials, credit card details, usernames and passwords;

- Launching DDoS or distributed denial of service denying legitimate users from accessing the sites of the service provider.

Usually, botmasters earn huge amounts from spammers when they send spam email messages via their botnets. Within the botnet, each computer may be sending only 10 messages at a time, which might not cause any alarms to be triggered. However, 10 thousand zombie computers acting as a botnet can send a million messages.

Once inside the network of the organization, it is easy for the attacker to steal identity information, details of credit cards, credentials of the individual users and usernames and passwords to sensitive sites such as banking and investments. With certain types of malware, the botmaster is able to monitor keystrokes of the users in the botnet and harvest their personal information. Among other things, the botmaster can even hijack the internet browser the user is working with.

The attacker or the botmaster can cripple entire websites and disallow legitimate users from reaching their targeted sites. Botnets can be used to create overwhelming traffic to a specific website, which clogs all the routes. This action maintains a DDoS attack until the website owner agrees to some demands from the botmaster.

HOW TO KNOW IF BOTNETS HAVE ATTACKED YOU

There are a few obvious signs that your computer has been co-opted by a botnet:

- The computer occasionally fails to respond to commands, crashes often and/or runs unusually slow;

- The internet or tnetwork connection is unusually slow;

- Even when you are not using the internet, there is considerable network activity;

- The computer is unable to access websites;

- There is a dramatic increase in the amount of spam you receive or generate;

- Your firewall occasionally alerts you about unknown processes and/or programs as they try to access the Internet.

HOW TO INSULATE COMPUTERS AGAINST BOTNETS

If you suspect your computer is showing signs of being hijacked as a botnet, you must download and run a malicious software detection tool, and scan for botnet infection.

If there is positive confirmation that your computer is indeed affected, you have the choice of removing it by yourself or enlisting the help of a computer security expert. To do it yourself, you will need to:

- Procure and install antimalware and antivirus software, and/or update your existing software;

- Use special removal tools such as AntiBot or RUBotted;

- Quarantine and delete any malware detected by these tools;

- Repeatedly scan your computer until all traces of malware are removed and there is no further symptom of botnet activity exhibited by your computer.

Once you have cleaned out your system, make sure you have an updated operating system, up-to-date application programs and a strong firewall alerting you whenever any process or program tries to access the internet.

REFERENCES:

1. Wallace, J., TopTen Reviews, *Botnet Zombie Apocalypse: How to Protect Your Computer.* Available from: <http://mac-internet-security-software-review.toptenreviews.com/how-do-i-know-if-my-computer-is-a-botnet-zombie-.html>. [2013].

2. Kilpatrik, I., Federation Against Software Theft, *BOTNETS AND HOW TO DEAL WITH THEM.* Available from: <http://www.fastiis.org/kaleidoscope/article/id/555/botnets-and-how-to-deal-with-them/>. [April 2010].

3. Microsoft, Safety & Security Center, *How to better protect your PC from botnets and malware.* Available from: <http://www.microsoft.com/security/pc-security/botnet.aspx>. [2013].

3

CAN FINANCIAL INSTITUTIONS OVERCOME THE NEPHOPHOBIA OF A CLOUD SECURITY BARRIER?

WHAT IS NEPHOPHOBIA IN THE CONTEXT OF CLOUD COMPUTING?

Nephophobia, in psychology, is used to describe a person's fear of clouds (in the sky). Financial institutions have an innate fear of cloud computing, with respect to the sensitive nature of their business transactions.

Things look terrifying when we do not understand them and are unable to figure out what they may be capable of doing to us. This fear is the main reason organizations also tend to maintain a safe distance when it comes to cloud computing.

WHY ARE FINANCIAL INSTITUTIONS HESITANT IN ADOPTING CLOUD COMPUTING?

The banking and securities sector is predicted to spend close to $84 billion on IT by 2016,making this sector the biggest IT buyer among all verticals, with insurance being the fourth. Although banks and other financial services appreciate the advantages that information technology has brought them at present, and will bring in the future, they see cloud computing as a different ball-game altogether. This makes financial institutions more cautious when adopting cloud computing. The major barriers that crop up in front of these financial institutions are:

- Control of cloud and risk of data; if the environment is of low trust, how can data be controlled and still be under complex regulatory frameworks?

- Given that data is under protection in the cloud, how can applications extract value from data without exposing it to the low trust system?

- Is it possible to retain control over data, giving the requirements of residency and legal search requests to the cloud provider, at the same time handing control back to the data owner?

Since these are very real issues, industry regulators have issued cloud guidance to enterprises addressing the regulatory risks stemming from the security concern in the cloud. The guidance should make organizations think carefully about their need to maximize values from information in the cloud, without a corresponding increase in regulatory compliance.

HOW CAN CLOUD COMPUTING SECURITY BARRIERS BE OVERCOME?

Financial institutions must ask for and rely on proofs. They should trust only independent validation of the approach, and reject anything else; for example, new data security standards such as FFX mode, AES[3], and NIST Format Preserving Encryption, which have the foundation of security proof and support of the standard body. Two methods of solving the risk of data and compliance barriers are:

- Data protection via a data-centric approach in the enterprise cloud stack;

- Data masking and de-identification in tandem with authorization, authentication and identity service layers.

Financial institutions need a solid understanding of the cloud services and deployment of proper architecture and business processes tuned to the requirements of IT security.

One way to tackle and overcome this security barrier is to confront it head-on. Management has to be made more comfortable with the cloud phenomenon. Selecting a partner who provides a friendly financial sector cloud service and deploying that for a non-critical part of the business could be a suitable starting point.

REFERENCES:

1. Bower, M., Help Net Security, *How financial institutions can overcome the cloud security barrier*. Available from: <http://www.net-security.org/article.php?id=1831>. [18 April 2013].

2. Dorf, M., HPC, *Overcoming the Cloud Security Barrier for Financial Services*. Available from: <http://www.hpcinthecloud.com/hpccloud/2013-05-10/overcoming_the_cloud_security_barrier_for_financial_services.html>. [10 May 2013].

3. Mahboubi, O., Asia Cloud Computing Association, *Nephophobia in Financial Institutions*. Available from: <http://www.asiacloud.org/index.php/2012-07-17-08-34-11/nephophobia-in-financial-institutions>. [2013].

4 | CLOUD HACKS: WHAT IS IT AND HOW TO PROTECT YOUR INFORMATION

WHAT IS CLOUD HACKING?

To know what Cloud Hacks are, we need to first understand what Cloud Computing is. Cloud Computing is a conglomeration of services such as:

- storage services
- web services
- spam filtering
- platform as a service
- utility–style infrastructure
- managed service providers
- software as a service
- service commerce platforms
- internet integration

Today, we use such cloud-based interconnections without much of it being in evidence; for example, Gmail, where we keep even our most intimate e-mails. In fact, most IT customers today plug into several isolated clouds of service individually. For example, we log on to different websites to read the news, to do our financial transactions and to read our mails. In the enterprise, increasing use of virtualization and Service Oriented Architecture (SOA) is creating the idea of loosely coupled services that run on agile and scalable infrastructure, eventually making the enterprise as a whole a node in the cloud.

However, all this comes at a price. With the proliferation of cloud services and cloud-connected devices, users now access data from beyond the firewall. This demands a shift in the way we secure data. Now, security is no longer confined to locking down the perimeter, it is about understanding who is accessing what information and whether they are allowed to do so. This calls for implementing an identity-centric approach to data security, and this is where the problem starts.

According to a recent Ponemon study, less than 30% of the organizations surveyed said they were confident about authentication of cloud users. That leaves a huge gap for attackers bent on usurping the identity of users and using it to clandestinely steal sensitive information, financial data and other important data. This in essence, is Cloud Hacking.

HOW TO PROTECT YOUR ENTERPRISE FROM CLOUD HACKING

Most people believe that data stored in remote servers or cloud services are inherently safe, as the cloud service provider would be watching over them. While that may be partly true, that does not absolve the owner of the data from taking his own safeguards to protect his data. After all, loss of data, for whatever reasons, would be a primary loss to the owner, and possibly only a secondary loss to others (the cloud service provider). Therefore, it is imperative that the data-owner assumes prime responsibility in backing up his data in multiple locations other than his main cloud service.

Even as cloud computing opens up vast opportunities for individuals and organizations, it also opens up security soft spots for data thieves and cybercriminals. Although cloud service providers may not be lax in providing security arrangements for keeping data safe, the same cannot be said for users of the service. Many simply do not understand or are unclear about their privacy settings.

One of the best ways of protecting data is to encrypt the whole thing. With encryption, you turn all data into something unintelligible, and it remains this way to anyone who does not have access to the keys that will unlock the content. Now, just like your login information, how you protect the encryption keys is critical to the safety and security of your data.

NEVER PLACE ALL YOUR EGGS IN ONE BASKET

Use different passwords for every single on-line account. Password management is not very difficult with the use of services such as LastPass or RoboForm, and you can even use them to generate hard-to-guess passwords. Additionally, never link all your sensitive accounts together through your passwords.

REFERENCES:

1. Sutter, J.D., CNN, How to protect your cloud data from hacks. Available from: <http://edition.cnn.com/2012/08/09/tech/web/cloud-security-tips>. [9 August 2012].

2. Hackenberger, B., USA Today, Encryption can make cloud computing safer. Available from: <http://www.usatoday.com/story/cybertruth/2013/05/31/cloud-security-hacking-encryption/2375689/>. [31 May 2013].

3. Mann, A., GreenPages, Cloud Security: From Hacking the Mainframe to Protecting Identity. Available from: <http://www.journeytothecloud.com/cloud-computing/cloud-security-from-hacking-the-mainframe-to-protecting-identity/>. [11 April 2013].

4. Knorr, E., Infoworld, What cloud computing really means. Available from: <http://www.infoworld.com/d/cloud-computing/what-cloud-computing-really-means-031>. [2011].

5

CRIME OVERCOMES ENCRYPTED SESSIONS OF MAJOR BROWSERS

Meta Description: *Major browsers use sessions that, although encrypted, allow attackers to decrypt the user's sessions*

WHAT IS CRIME?

Servers use HTTP Secure or HTTPS traffic to encrypt user authentication cookies. For this, they use the Transport Layer Security or TLS, Secure Socket Layer or SSL, and a protocol named SPDY (pronounced Speedy), which decrypts the cookies that the user sends for authentication. The CRIME attack exploits the data compression scheme to collect information about the user.

HOW IS A CRIME ATTACK DONE?

CRIME uses brute force to remember authenticated users by decrypting the HTTPS cookies that the website sets. Usually, a website returns cookies that authenticate the user when the user sends their credentials to the website. The CRIME attack code, planted as a malware in the user's computer, forces the browser used by the victim to send specially modified HTTPS requests to the targeted website. Once the request is compressed and returned by the server, CRIME analyzes them to determine the value of the cookie for the session.

WHAT HAPPENS DURING A CRIME ATTACK?

Once the cookie is decoded, the attacker can return to the site visited by the user and login using the collected credentials. The attacker masquerading as the authentic user may steal important information. Without the knowledge of the user, fraudulent financial transactions may steal money from bank accounts.

Attackers plant a JavaScript code in the user's computer. This code runs when the user works with his browser. The code sniffs or analyzes the victim's HTTPS traffic, and decrypts session cookies. The attack succeeds only if both the client and the server support the data compression-decompression feature used by the SSL/TLS/SPDY.

Almost all servers use SSL and TLS for rendering their HTTPS traffic, however, Google and Firefox use SPDY, also a networking protocol with compression, multiplexing and prioritization for reducing the time that web pages take to load. SPDY does not actually replace either HTTP or HTTPS, but it helps to speed up data transfer.

The culprit is the compression technique or algorithm that SSL, TLS and SPDY use. This algorithm, DEFLATE, eliminates duplicate strings. The algorithm replaces repeated strings with a small token on each request and the length of the request will reduce with each repeat request.

CRIME analyzes the difference in consecutive requests to guess the value of the cookie. By repeatedly sending requests to the server, it tries to regenerate the information that is being encrypted. Although it is not possible to directly read the session cookie that is included in the requests as the browser uses many security mechanisms, CRIME controls the path of each new request by inserting different strings into the request and attempting to match the value of the cookie.

Even though session cookies can be long and may contain digits, lowercase letters and uppercase letters, special algorithms in CRIME help to avoid making a large number of requests for decrypting them. Sometimes CRIME requires only four requests and at the most six may be needed.

HOW TO PREVENT SUCCESSFUL CRIME

CRIME needs to plant the JavaScript code into the victim's computer for the attack to be fruitful. Therefore, the user has to protect his system and network from an outside attack and also an inside attack. Anti-malware, anti-spyware and anti-virus software programs must be used and the network hardened with proper security systems such as firewalls and security policies.

For CRIME to succeed, both the server and the client should be using the same compression/decompression techniques/protocols. Using the latest versions of browsers mitigates the problem, as many have patched up their code and are no longer using the compression algorithms. Google has modified SPDY to avoid attacks from CRIME.

REFERENCES:

1. Fisher, D., Threat Post, *New Attack Uses SSL/TLS Information Leak to Hijack HTTPS Sessions.* Available from: <http://threatpost.com/new-attack-uses-ssltls-information-leak-hijack-https-sessions-090512/>. [5 September 2012].

2. Constantin, L., ComputerWorld, *'CRIME' attack abuses SSL/TLS data compression feature to hijack HTTPS sessions.* Available from: <http://news.idg.no/cw/art.cfm?id=976ED08F-CB4A-23DA-FFDA0419B8750B72>. [14 September 2012].

3. Goodin, D., ARS Technica, *Crack in Internet's foundation of trust allows HTTPS session hijacking.* Available from: <http://arstechnica.com/security/2012/09/crime-hijacks-https-sessions/>. [13 September 2011].

6

NETWORK DEVICES AND SECURE CONFIGURATION

WHAT HAPPENS IF NETWORK DEVICES DO NOT HAVE A SECURE CONFIGURATION?

When in normal use, secured configuration for network devices gradually become less securely configured. This happens as users demand exceptions for temporary and/or specific business requirements and as the exceptions are deployed. Over time, those exceptions are never closed even after the business need has ceased to be applicable.

In many cases, the security risk arising from the exclusion is not correctly analyzed. In addition, the risk is not evaluated against the related business need and changes over time.

The less securely configured network devices such as switches, routers and firewalls have electronic holes in them, which the attackers target and use to penetrate the defense.

Through the flaws of these network devices, the attacker not only gains control of target networks, but also is able to redirect the traffic on the network to another compromised system impersonating as a trusted unit. This system is then used to intercept information during transmission and alter it.

Network devices that are not securely configured allow the attacker to gain access to sensitive and critical data, and the attacker then alters or steals the important information.

EFFECTS ON THE ORGANIZATION

Business continuity of an organization depends primarily on the availability of network, with network configuration data being the core of enterprise network administration.

Network device configuration is crucial to network security, as the network devices they control provide access to credentials, access control lists, SNMP settings and many other sensitive data.

Neglecting the crucial aspects of network configuration management and device administration management leads to disaster for the organization, should an attacker gain access to the vulnerable network devices.

HOW TO COMBAT THE THREAT MOST EFFECTIVELY

Implement ingress and egress filtering at network interconnection points such as at inter-organization connections, Internet gateways and all internal network segments that have different security controls. Allow only the protocols and ports which have an explicit and documented business need. Block all other protocols and ports with rules that de-fault-deny. Use the routers, network-based IPS and firewalls to accomplish this.

Use commercial tools that will continuously evaluate the rule set for network filtering devices and decide whether they are consistent or in conflict. This provides automated sanity checks for network filters.

Compare the configuration of all switches, routers and fire-walls against the standard secure configuration that is de-fined for each type of network device the organization uses. An organization change control board must document, re-view and approve the security configurations of all network devices. A change control system must document and ap-prove any deviation from the standard configurations.

Configure the system in such a manner that it can identify any changes to the network devices. This must include all IPS and IDS based systems, firewalls, switches and routers. The changes that the system should be capable of identify-ing must include software installed on the device, configura-tion files, ports, services and modification to key files.

REFERENCES:

1. Mullen, T., ComputerWeekly.com., *How to combat the Sans Institute's top 10 security threats*. Available from: <http://www.computerweekly.com/opinion/How-to-combat-the-Sans-Institutes-top-10-security-threats>. [January 2008].

2. Bala, V., Manage Engine PitStop, *Why should you care about streamlining the management of network device configs and passwords?* Available from: <http://blogs.manageengine.com/passwordmanagerpro/2013/03/11/a-better-way-to-manage-the-configurations-and-passwords-of-network-devices.html>. [11 March 2013].

3. The SANS Institute, *Critical Control 10: Secure Configurations for Network Devices such as Firewalls, Routers, and Switches.* Available from: <http://www.sans.org/critical-security-controls/control.php?id=10>. [2013].

7 | YOUR BUSINESS CRITICAL APPLICATIONS ARE VULNERABLE TO SSRF ATTACKS

WHAT ARE BUSINESS CRITICAL SYSTEMS AND WHAT IS AN SSRF ATTACK?

Modern businesses run on business application infrastructure, with typical modules such as Enterprise Resource Planning or ERP, Customer Relationship Management or CRM and Supplier Relationship Management or SRM. These systems hold data related to personnel, financial and other sensitive information critical to the operation of the enterprise. Moreover, these systems are often connected to the Supervisory Control and Data Acquisition systems (SCADA) and/or banking client workstations.

Server Side Request Forgery or SSRF is an attack on existing vulnerability of the business application infrastructure. Attackers use a victim server interface that can send a packet to another host on another port and can be accessed remotely without authentication.

WHAT HAPPENS DURING AN SSRF ATTACK?

Business-critical systems are usually located in a secure sub-network secured by firewalls and monitored by Intrusion Detection Systems, regularly patched for their vulnerabilities.

The ERP and other networks are usually separated from the corporate networks by a firewall. In turn, the corporate networks are protected from the Internet and cloud systems by another firewall. However, insecure systems have vulnerabilities existing between the corporate network and the ERP network, which attackers exploit.

During an SSRF attack, a compromised server sends a packet to a service, which then encloses another packet within the original packet and forwards it to another service. It is much like sending a forged letter hidden inside another letter. Much depends on how much the attacker can manipulate the contents of the second packet and that constitutes different types of SSRF attacks. There are typically two types of SSRF attacks: Trusted and Remote.

The trusted SSRF attacks can usually send forged packets or forged requests to predefined services. Remote SSRF attacks involve forged requests to any remote port or IP.

Trusted SSRF attacks are very stealthy, as most of the systems across the enterprise are linked through the secure sub network, and the behavior of the requests looks very normal. However, these attacks are somewhat difficult to make because they need an existing link and credentials such as usernames and passwords.

On the other hand, remote SSRF attacks are possible from a trusted source to any host and any port, even if the source cannot connect to the remote hosts directly. Attackers scan the remote hosts for open ports and IP addresses. If authentication is not required, it is possible to scan an internal network from the Internet. Remote SSRF threats can:

- Exploit Operating System and Data Base vulnerabilities
- Exploit the vulnerabilities of old ERP applications
- Bypass the security restrictions of ERP
- Exploit existing vulnerabilities in ERP local services

WHY IS AN SSRF ATTACK CRITICAL TO THE ENTERPRISE?

The company's critical information is stored in its ERP and this makes the attack on the ERP system very lucrative to a competitor, an industrial spy or a cybercriminal. The critical information may include intellectual property, information on public or customer relations, personally identifiable information and most importantly, financial data.

A business can suffer a significant amount of damage if the ERP system is compromised due to insider embezzlement, fraud, sabotage or industrial espionage.

HOW TO PREVENT SSRF ATTACKS

Most business critical systems require close collaborations with the vendor to close the vulnerabilities allowing SSRF attacks. Regular patching and use of continuous monitoring systems along with vulnerability assessment systems will help. It is preferable to use systems that can expose zero-day vulnerabilities.

Let application security experts assess the business critical systems and monitor the systems with automated solutions such as ERPScan Security Scanner. The scanner can identify misconfigurations, vulnerabilities, and many other issues.

REFERENCES:

1. Polyakov, A., *SSRF vs. Business critical applications.* Available from: <http://media.blackhat.com/bh-us-12/Briefings/Polyakov/BH_US_12_Polyakov_SSRF_Business_WP.pdf>. [?].

2. Polyakov, A., *SSRF: The new threat for business – critical applications.* Available from: <http://erpscan.com/wp-content/uploads/2012/09/SSRF-The-new-threat-for-business-critical-applications-from-RSA.pdf>. [2012].

3. Polyakov, A., *SSRF attacks in the limelight at ERPScan's press conference in China.* Available from: <http://erpscan.com/press-center/news/ssrf-attacks-in-the-limelight-at-erpscans-press-conference-in-china/>. [17 September 2012].

8

THE EFFECTS OF BLENDED THREATS AND JAVASCRIPT

WHAT IS A BLENDED THREAT AND JAVASCRIPT?

A blended threat is a single threat that carries multiple vectors inside to cause further damage. A malicious JavaScript containing multiple malware, Trojans, etc. within, can hijack a web browser and exploit further vulnerabilities inside. The multiple vectors may target the host, disable the security software and download more worms, Trojans and backdoors. These could be used to further control the now hijacked machine, such as sending out spam and hosting web pages to cause further damage.

WHAT HAPPENS DURING A BLENDED THREAT ATTACK?

We have all visited free download sites that make us wait, say 30 seconds before the download starts, counting down as 29, 28, 27, etc. An attacker can couch his attack in a similar way and during the waiting time, change the password to the router, or upload new firmware. This allows the attacker to do whatever he wishes. Usually, this is sniffing the traffic for passwords and similar information, and forwarding them to the attacker's site.

A JavaScript attack blends cross-site scripting in a known application with vulnerabilities in application cookie security. This can also happen by exploiting human trust, requiring a user to enter their credentials into a malicious web page that is designed to mimic the original application.

With a successful attack, the attacker can gain access to sensitive information and or privilege escalation through additional vulnerabilities. The attacker can change the configuration of a device or the password of the administrator as well.

The attacker begins his attack on the internal networks by inducing the user to run a small JavaScript code initiated through the browser. Several different vectors may be used for this, for example, sites offering surveys, malicious Search Engine Optimization, social networks, media download sites and compromised ad networks.

A blended attack may also be used to discover the devices existing on the victim's network, and exploiting the vulnerabilities. The attacker can then achieve a persistent and most often a permanent network compromise.

To achieve a level of persistence, in which the attacker maintains access to a compromised device over long periods, the attacker may use C&C or botnet Command and Control systems.

Attackers mainly target Small Office Home Office (SOHO) routers since this affords them additional benefits. One of the benefits is the target is directly addressable from the

Internet. The attacker can then implement port-knocking techniques to sniff for pre-determined sequence of packets.

WHAT ARE THE RISKS FROM A BLENDED THREAT ATTACK?

With a permanent presence in a network, a whole world of possibilities opens up for the attacker. The level of function-ality gained after exploiting the network gives some idea of the extent of damage that is possible in the attack:

- Sniffing for passwords and credit card details
- Intercepting the network and replacing ad-network engines
- Pivoting on the network to attack other devices
- Propagating to other local networks and foreign net-works
- Denial of service for completely covert attacks
- Creating scalable bot-nets with the routers
- Creating a private VPN for the attacker
- Intercepting/manipulating traffic
- Inserting malicious JavaScript code to exploit further
- Poisoning the cache
- Attacking CDMA routers using JavaScript
- Remote dialing modems or cellular enabled routers

HOW CAN RISKS FROM BLENDED THREAT ATTACKS BE MITIGATED?

- Follow RFC-5735 and do not allow sites from the Internet to be able to access Private IP Addresses.

- Restrict Cross-Origin Resource Sharing for transferring large chunks of data to foreign domains

- Enable Cross Site Request Forgery protections on all embedded devices.

- Use embedded devices that support secure and automatic software updates.

- Limit the use of JavaScript in the enterprise as far as possible.

- Establish new heuristics to detect and respond to blended JavaScript and CSFU threats.

REFERENCES:

1. Appsec Conulting Inc., *Blended Threats and JavaScript: A Plan for Permanent Network Compromise*. Available from: <http://media.blackhat.com/bh-us-12/Briefings/Purviance/BH_US_12_Purviance_Blended_Threats_WP.pdf>. [1 July, 2012].

2. Kyukendall, D., *Blended Threats & JavaScript (OWASP AppSecUSA Presentation Review)*. Available from: <http://www.manvswebapp.com/blended-threats-javascript-plan-permanent-network-compromise>. [2013].

3. Fireeye, *Unraveling Web Malware*. Available from: <http://www.sarrelgroup.com/Documents/FE_unravel_web_malware_wp.pdf>. [2008].

9 | HOW TO AVOID PHISHING ATTACKS FROM TRUSTED THIRD PARTIES

WHAT IS PHISHING FROM TRUSTED THIRD PARTIES?

You may receive a message, purportedly sent by the National Credit Union Administration, with a request to click the provided link for updating your data. To enter the site, you have to enter your credentials, and this is the exact information the phisher wanted.

If the phishers have access to your bank account, they may withdraw money from your bank. However, this will leave an electronic trail, which is not very easy to get rid of and the law enforcement authorities will be in hot pursuit. Therefore, instead of cleaning out your bank account, the phishers prefer to sell your credentials to other fraudsters who operate with more sophistication and who can erase their trail when emptying your bank account.

Trusted third parties such as banks, e-auction and e-pay systems are the major targets that phishers use. They make a fake site that closely resembles the original. The user will generally not suspect anything amiss and they enter their username and password thinking they are accessing the original site.

In a similar way, phishers also target the use's email credentials, which they sell to other fraudsters who distribute viruses or create zombie networks.

DIFFERENT TRICKS THAT PHISHERS USE

Phishers use links, which they design to look very similar to the URLs of credible sites. Less experienced users are easily fooled by these links. More experienced users will be able to notice the difference and avoid clicking on them. Such fake links often begin with an IP address, which credible sites do not commonly use.

A phishing message may look like or imitate an eBay notification. Although the body of the message may contain a link to take the user to the legitimate site, the URL itself may be different. There may be other links to the official site, but the link that requires the user to enter their credentials will lead to the fake site.

A new trend has started on the Internet called 'Pharming'. Pharmers also target access credentials, and they obtain their data via official websites, unlike phishers who send emails to entice their victims.

Phishers mostly target financial sites such as PayPal, eBay and most of the banks. Although most phishing attacks are random, they can be targeted as well. For targeted attacks, fraudsters make certain that a user has an account in a certain bank, before they launch a targeted attack to gain his credentials for the bank site. Although the targeted method means more complications and greater expense for the phishers, the payoff is also higher, as there is a greater chance that the victim will be hooked.

Apart from identity theft, a phishing link may present a far more sinister threat. Phishers may be able to plant spyware, malware, a Trojan program or a key logger in the user's system, once they have the username and password of the victim. Therefore, even if the user does not have a bank account the phisher may steal, the user may not be entirely safe.

HOW TO PROTECT YOURSELF FROM PHISHING SCAMS

It is better to err on the side of caution. Unless you are absolutely confident of the genuineness of the email, it would be prudent to dismiss it as a fraud. Sending username, passwords, account numbers and any other confidential or personal information via email should be avoided at all times. Delete the email immediately (in case the phisher has also sent a malware along) and call the customer service of the sender of the email to verify the legitimacy.

You must use only the latest generation of web browsers. The latest IE and Firefox have built in protection against phishing, and your browser should be able to warn you against phishing and pharming attacks.

REFERENCES:

1. Tschabitscher, H., About.com Guide, *Phishing.* Available from: <http://email.about.com/od/ staysecureandprivate/g/phishing.htm>. [?].

2. Kaspersky Lab, *What is phishing?* Available from: <http:// www.securelist.com/en/threats/spam?chapter=85>. [2013].

3. Bradley, T., Internet/Network Security, *Protect Yourself From Phishing Scams.* Available from: <http://netsecu- rity.about.com/od/security101/a/phishprotect.htm>. [?].

10 ATTACKS VIA USB

WHAT IS AN ATTACK VIA USB?

Although USB devices help computer operators simpli-fy their storage and transfer problems in a myriad of ways, they are also the most common devices for delivery of malware.

The main process of malware delivery via USB happens because of the AutoRun feature in Windows, which allows any executable file on the USB device to be automatically detected and launched.

Any infected USB device, it could be a mobile phone, a flash drive, an mp3 player, digital camera or a PSP, can start an executable file, which then lets in a wide array of malware into the computer. The damaging malware then makes its way into the core of the Windows operating system, and begins replicating itself every time the computer restarts.

Although AutoRun is a very useful feature in Windows, it helps spread more than two-thirds of current malware. Thankfully, AutoPlay has replaced it. This feature asks the user if he/she would like to run the executable file it has detected on the USB device, and offers other choices such as opening the folder to view the files. A similar feature is available in Macintosh computers, and this is more secure than the Window's AutoRun. Linux straightaway displays the folders and has no AutoRun feature, making it somewhat safer than the other two. However, the threat from the USB devices goes deeper than AutoRun.

HOW DOES THE ATTACKER GAIN ACCESS VIA USB?

Attackers use the USB port in different ways for implementing their nefarious activities. One of the simpler ways is to let in an executable file through the AutoRun feature of Windows, or to entice the user to execute it when AutoPlay offers various choices. However, scanning the USB medium with an anti-virus or an anti-malware program can eliminate most malware if the AutoRun feature is turned off.

The other way attackers gain access is less obvious and there is really no easy method of stopping or preventing the attack. An attacker could be an insider, such as a disgruntled employee, intent on stealing information to pass on to a business competitor. The attacker attaches a USB dongle to the computer. This dongle sits between the keyboard and the computer, and all keystrokes the user makes, pass through the dongle. Since the dongle does not add any software to the computer, it remains undetected by the anti-virus and anti-malware programs. Being physically small and residing behind the computer, the dongle goes virtually undetected.

The dongle collects keystrokes the user makes and stores them in its memory. When the dongle is removed and the attacker analyzes it, he gains access to all the passwords and usernames of the owner of the computer. The attacker can then use this information any way he likes.

In some cases, the USB dongle masquerades as a keyboard and a mouse, and there is no way any anti-virus or anti-malware can block it. The user's keystrokes are surreptitiously passed to the attacker through the USB dongle via browser and internet connection. The attacker then has full control of the user's computer.

HOW TO PREVENT ATTACKS FROM THE USB

Unless you are sure of the USB device, **never start your computer with the USB device attached**. This accounts for 60% of malware to gain access to the computer before any anti-virus or anti-malware program can even start up.

Have a company-wide policy of allowing only permitted USB devices to operate on the computer. Other non-permitted USB devices will be detected and blocked. This is possible by altering the Registry in Windows and adding suitable scripts to Mac and Linux computers.

Have better security for physical access to sensitive computers and to their USB ports. Restricting access to the USB port eliminates this threat.

REFERENCES:

1. Savvas, M., Computerworld UK, *Cybercrooks Use USB Devices in Attacks*. Available from: <http://www.tech-hive.com/article/209853/cybercrooks_use_usb_devices_in_attacks.html>. [7 November 2010].

2. Caroll, S., PC Mag.com, *USB Malware Attacks On the Rise*. Available from: <http://www.pcmag.com/article2/0,2817,2372152,00.asp>. [4 November 2010].

3. Mills, E., CNET, *Researchers turn USB cable into attack tool*. Available from: <http://news.cnet.com/8301-27080_3-20028919-245.html>. [19 January 2011].

4. Beccaonline.org, *The Evolution of USB Based Microcontroller Attacks in Corporate Espionage*. Available from: <http://www.becca-online.org/images/The_Evolution_of_USB_Based_Microcontroller_Attacks_in_Corporate_Espionage.pdf>. [?].

5. Crenshaw, A., Irongeek.com, *Plug and Prey: Malicious USB Devices*. Available from: <http://www.irongeek.com/i.php?page=security/plug-and-prey-malicious-usb-devices>. [2011].

11 | OVERCOMING SEVERE DDOS ATTACKS

WHAT IS A DDOS ATTACK?

Servers have finite resources to handle traffic. When you log in for a specific service, and are unable to access the website, the server may have possibly run out of resources to handle the necessary traffic. A source or a system may have attacked the server denying access to genuine users by flooding all the resources of the server with repeated requests or the server may have been compromised into denying access to its legitimate users. This is a Denial of Service or DoS attack.

On the other hand, when the denial of service originates from hundreds of thousands of systems or nodes, the attack can be extremely severe, sophisticated and well coordinated. Because of the enhanced scale of the attack and its distributed nature, this type of attack is called Distributed Denial of Service or DDoS.

The node and controller system in a DDoS attack is called a "bot". A network of bots is called the "botnet" and the 'botmasters' control the bots in the botnet either with a direct port connection between the computers or through the Internet Relay Chat. They compromise servers around the world, link them up and with a few commands, can instruct the infected nodes to attack a target.

There are two major types of DDoS attacks. In the first type of attack, attackers flood the connectivity link with an aim to saturate the bandwidth. The other type is the packet-based attack, which seeks to overwhelm the processing capability of the target equipment. All equipment, routers and switches included, have a finite capability and face a hard time when they have to handle packets far in excess of their capacity.

WHY DO DDOS ATTACKS TAKE PLACE?

DDoS usually has social dynamics leading to the attack. They do not occur randomly. Rather, they are targeted and have a motive. Although the motive could be revenge, most of the time the motive is financial. Most of the time, attackers are hired for the job, and they are paid for meticulously executing an untraceable attack.

DDoS attackers usually contact their victims via a phone call, a post or an email, and instigate an altercation. This is followed by a negative reaction finally escalating to a situation of attack. Although DDoS perpetrators hire the attackers, prices vary from a few dollars per hour for a simple non-distributed DoS attack to several hundred dollars per hour for a sophisticated DDoS attack. The attackers are asked to "drop" a certain website or a network off the Internet.

That the DDoS attack is mostly hired, is a blessing in disguise, as the attack wears out when the client runs out of funds to support the attack. If the target can sustain the

attack with perseverance, a DoS or a DDoS attack is likely to fizzle out over time.

HOW TO LEARN ABOUT BOTS AND HOW TO COUNTER THE THREAT OF DDOS

Botnets can be of immense size, with tens of thousands of systems linked together. By logging data over time, it is possible to reconstruct the actions of the attackers and study the tools they use. For discovering the motives of the attackers, their tactics and their tools, new techniques such as honeypots/honeynets are being used.

By studying the attack methods, it is possible to locate the existing loopholes in the protocols. Counter measures can then be taken to strengthen the system against possible attacks. This means modifying the system configuration to eliminate the possibility of accepting a DDoS attack and guarding against illegitimate traffic. The main strategies for detection involve anomaly detection, signature detection and hybrid systems.

By using up-to-date protocols and software, the computer's weaknesses can be cured. It is also necessary to scan the machine regularly to weed out any "anomalous" behavior. System security mechanisms can include monitoring the physical access to the computer and its applications, installing the latest security patches, virus scanners, firewall systems and automatic intrusion detection systems.

REFERENCES:

1. CISCO, The Internet Protocol Journal - Volume 7, Number 4, *Distributed Denial of Service Attacks.* Available from: <http://www.cisco.com/web/about/ac123/ac147/archived_issues/ipj_7-4/dos_attacks.html>. [December 2004].

2. Unixy, *The penultimate guide to stopping a DDoS attack – A new approach.* Available from: <http://blog.unixy.net/2010/08/the-penultimate-guide-to-stopping-a-ddos-attack-a-new-approach/>. [24 March 2011].

3. Bacher, P., *Know your Enemy: Tracking Botnets.* Available from: <http://www.honeynet.org/book/export/html/50>. [?].

12

HOW ATTACKERS ACHIEVE PERMANENT BACKDOORING OF HTML5 CLIENT-SIDE APPLICATIONS AND AFFECT YOUR SECURITY

WHAT IS PERMANENT BACKDOORING OF HTML5 CLIENT-SIDE APPLICATIONS?

Websites improve the performance of mobile users by using the HTML5 local storage and caching app logic on the client devices. For example, many websites embed third-party widgets, which are a security risk for companies that use such services. Attackers may exploit such local storage caches to create permanent backdoors in these applications.

WHAT HAPPENS IF A CLIENT-SIDE APPLICATION IS EXPLOITED?

Local storage is a common feature of HTML5, and classified as such. It offers a method of saving content on the device of the visitor, and affords more flexibility and larger space than some of the earlier methods such as cookies. Such local storage offers additional benefits to the server, that of code caching.

As web pages routinely require larger blocks of JavaScript, they avoid downloading the code each time the visitor returns to the site. Instead, they save a copy on the local storage of the user. This provides a significant performance boost for a mobile user, who is limited by bandwidth and for whom cookies may not be as useful.

For the attacker, this method has opened new possibilities for compromising the local storage. By injecting a malicious code into the local storage, they open a backdoor that remains on the client-side cache or is persistent. Every time the user visits the site and executes the app, the code delivers its payload and is not affected by closing the browser. Detecting the attack is usually difficult, as the user may not even be aware of anything mischievous happening.

Some advertisements offer a "like" button similar to those on social networking sites such as Facebook and Twitter. This is one of the ways for malicious JavaScript code to transfer itself from the infected site to a user's local storage. Selecting the "like" button on a web page transfers the third-party JavaScript code on the page to the user's local storage. Since the code has the same capabilities as other scripts on the page, the attacker can very easily transfer a malicious code such as XSS into the local storage.

With the resident code in place, an attacker has complete control over the web client. He can access the web application acting as if he were the attacked user, in short, impersonate the user. The attacker now controls all web traffic (to and from) between the user and the web application. The server has no way of recognizing the attack, and even if it did, it has no way of informing the user.

The exploit can have countless different attack payloads. Some of the more common payloads are:

- Stealing session cookies;
- Inducing the user to give up their credentials;
- Injecting Trojans into the system;
- Stealing data such as from the autocomplete cache a
- Logging keystrokes

IS THERE ANY PROTECTION AGAINST SUCH ATTACKS?

The major problem with this is sort of attack is it is not caused by avulnerability, but by a feature that brings convenience. Preventing such attacks is possible through protecting the web pages against manipulation of XSS vulnerability and malicious advertisements. Although this is good enough for the server side, the client side needs more considerations.

To be on the safe side, do not use any user-controlled parameters until you have checked them for malicious content.. If you must, accept only those that you know are safe, whitelist them and blacklist all others.

If you are already infected, the following steps will likely provide a solution:

- Close all browser windows leaving only one open;
- Close all tabs in the open window leaving only one;
- In this open tab, call about:blank;
- Delete all data the web application may have stored, including cookies, caches, etc.;
- Restart the browser;
- Alternately, delete the profile of the browser.

REFERENCES:

1. Tyson, J., Gemini Security Solutions, *How a Platform Using HTML5 Can Affect the Security of Your Website.* Available from: <http://securitymusings.com/article/3159/how-a-platform-using-html5-can-affect-the-security-of-your-website>. [1 February 2012].

2. Eilers, C, CtoVision, *HTML5 Security: Learn more about two of many new attacks.* Available from: <http://ctovision.com/2013/04/learn-more-about-two-of-many-new-attacks-html5-security/>. [29 April 2013].

3. Anley, C., The Web Application, *Chapter 2 – Core Defense Mechanisms.* Available from: <http://mdsec.net/wahh/answers2e.html>. [2011].

13 | HOW TO BLOCK ZERO-DAY APPLICATION EXPLOITS

WHAT IS A ZERO-DAY APPLICATION EXPLOIT?

Cyber criminals develop newer methods of bypassing security controls when installing malware on corporate endpoints. For example, the newly discovered APT or Advanced Persistent Threat malware uses multiple evasion techniques for bypassing many of the latest detection approaches being utilized. The malware executes only when there is some mouse activity. This action helps it to avoid being detected in the first stage.

In a zero-day exploit, the malware takes advantage of security vulnerability before the weakness becomes known, or on the same day that the vulnerability is discovered. There can be many zero days between initial discovery of the vulnerability and the first attack, before the vulnerability is patched.

WHAT HAPPENS IN A ZERO-DAY APPLICATION EXPLOIT?

In general, the discovery of a potential security issue in a software program leads to a notification to the software company, and in most cases, to the world at large. The software company takes some time to fix its code, before it is ready to distribute a software update or a patch. Even if a potential attacker becomes aware of the vulnerability, it would take him some time to exploit the issue. Meanwhile, hopefully, the software company will make the fix available first.

However, sometimes the attacker is the first to discover the vulnerability. Since no one else knows about the vulnerability, there is obviously no guard against it being exploited.

Blacklisting usually fails in such cases, because cyber criminals keep changing their tactics to avoid detection. Enterprises trying to use application control or whitelisting find to their dismay that it is nearly impossible to control, as the whitelist becomes very large. The number of files they need to review and validate is extraordinarily large, significantly delaying the deployment.

HOW CAN ZERO-DAY APPLICATION EXPLOITS BE KEPT UNDER CONTROL?

The following methods are recommended to prevent enterprises from being exposed to zero-day application exploits:

- Using IPsec or virtual LANs for protecting contents of individual transmissions;
- Deploying an intrusion detection system;

- Introducing network access control for preventing malicious machines from gaining access to the network;

- Locking down the wireless access points and using a security scheme such as WPA2 or Wi-Fi Protected Access for providing maximum protection against wireless-based attacks.

An endpoint malware protection paradigm helps by controlling malware from reaching the endpoint device and installing itself. Even if the malware is able to bypass the security successfully, the enterprise must have detection programs in place to prevent it from functioning.

Advanced data-stealing malware can be stopped from reaching the endpoint devices by new approaches such as the Stateful Application Control. This has two components: the first prevents malware from installing itself on the device; the second prevents malware from executing on the device. The application exploit prevention, as the first layer is called, is an application of whitelisting to the application states, rather than to the applications themselves.

REFERENCES:

1. Rouse, M., Search Security, *zero-day exploit.* Available from: <http://searchsecurity.techtarget.com/definition/zero-day-exploit>. [July 2010].

2. Tamir, D., Business security, *Can we end zero-day exploits?* Available from: <http://biztechreport.co.uk/2013/04/can-we-end-zero-day-exploits/>. [14 April 2013].

3. Tubin, G., Help Net Security, *Blocking zero-day application exploits*: *A new approach for APT prevention.* Available from: <http://www.net-security.org/article.php?id=1824>. [3 April 2013].

14

MANAGING DATA PRIVACY AND REPELLING ATTACKS ON ODATA

WHAT IS DATA PRIVACY AND WHAT IS ODATA?

Whenever people collect uniquely identifiable information in any form relating to a person, there can be privacy problems. Privacy issues can be a result of non-existent or improper disclosure control. Around the world, the right-to-privacy and right-to-data-privacy vary a great deal and so does their legal protection.

Although privacy and security are related, they may not necessarily mean the same thing. For example, an enterprise may take several measures to implement information security, but still not be able to protect the privacy of data.

The fundamental aspect of the problem lies in the way data protection is applied; protection is usually effected at the container level. The container could be a database, a server, or a directory within a file system. Protection is usually not applied at the granular level of data, which results in the control of ownership remaining at the container level, and not with the data subject itself. Therefore, when there is a data transfer, usually from one container to another, the data subject loses track of the data.

The OData or the Open Data Protocol is an open web protocol. People use it for querying and updating data in their databases. With OData, you can create HTTP-based RESTful data services and use it to edit and publish resources. You can use OData to expose and access information from a variety of sources such as traditional websites, content management systems, file systems, relational databases and many more.

With OData, a consumer can use HTTP protocol to query a database and receive back the results in formats such as plain XML, JSON[4] or Atom.

WHAT ARE THE RISKS INVOLVING ODATA?

The protocol used by OData does not include security specifications. Rather it suggests the implementations of what the user finds best fit for their target scenario. Moreover, as the OData protocol uses HTTP, JSON and AtomPub, it is susceptible to the security considerations relevant to each of those technologies. The most common risks involved with the use of OData are:

- Accessibility to the service document;
- Unrestricted data access through feed URIs[5] ;
- Accessibility to the Service Metadata Document;
- Enumeration of feeds using the Service Metadata Document;

- Attack on template creation process through use of Oyedata;

- Use of insecure HTTP verbs such as PUT, DELETE, POST and GET.

Apart from the above, there are other concerns such as HTTP verb tunneling, which the OData protocol offers for working with clients that do not support HTTP verbs like MERGE, PUT or DELETE. The concern is use of such verbs may be prohibited as direct invocation on some resources, but execution may be allowed via X-HTTP-Method header.

In a relational database, navigation from one entity to another may be allowed via a relationship. It is possible to access the navigation property by appending the name of the property to a single entity.

HOW TO MITIGATE THE SECURITY RISKS WHEN USING ODATA

Test an OData implementation for various data validation scenarios depending on the type of backend system it talks to. To provide exhaustive test coverage, use injection attacks and other relevant data validation tests as applicable.

Send incomplete data types and malformed XML and JSON request formats to make sure the system has proper error handling schemes. Do not allow invalid entries to render the database unusable.

Create a unique key for each new entry inserted into the database. The uniqueness of the keys must be strictly enforced through proper checks. **Non-unique keys may ultimately lead to a corrupt database.**

REFERENCES:

1. Kalra, G.S., McAfee, *A Pentester's Guide to Hacking Odata.* Available from: <http://www.mcafee.com/us/resources/white-papers/foundstone/wp-pentesters-guide-to-hacking-odata.pdf>. [2012].

2. Jericho Forum, *Principles for Managing Data Privacy.* Available from: <http://docs.media.bitpipe.com/io_10x/io_102267/item_465972/whitepaper_75712573870.pdf>. [May 2007].

3. Kalra, G. S., McAfee, *Attacking Odata.* Available from: <https://media.blackhat.com/ad-12/Kalra/bh-ad-12-Oyedata-Kalra-slides.pdf>. [2012].

15 | THWARTING CLICKJACKING AND CROSS-SITE SCRIPTING ATTACKS

WHAT IS CLICKJACKING?

You may have clicked on an innocent looking button on a web page that promised it would show you how fluffy the new kitty looked. However, you are taken instead to 'liking' something that you normally would not, and you know that your click has been hijacked or that you have been the victim of clickjacking.

HOW CLICKJACKING AFFECTS YOU?

Attackers create web pages with invisible buttons hidden on top of normal looking buttons. Users are tricked into clicking on the visible button, but in reality, they are actually clicking the invisible button. The invisible button is actually a link to something that the attacker wants done. This could be -

- Tricking you into changing the privacy settings on your Facebook account;

- Tricking you into 'liking' something that you normally would not like;

- Tricking you into becoming a Twitter follower for an unknown user;

- Tricking you into enabling the microphone or camera in your computer.

Clickjacking can have more serious consequences than those listed above. As clickjackers will usually load up a legitimate website within a frame and finally overlay their invisible button on top, they can take you to places that can spell disaster for you.

Consider a clickjacker using your bank's webpage on which he has overlaid his invisible button. He asks you to click there for additional safety. When you click, you are asked to enter your username and password. While you think you are entering your details into the legitimate website of your bank, in reality, you are only handing over your personal details to the clickjacker. With these details, there is nothing the attacker cannot do.

WHAT IS CROSS-SITE SCRIPTING?

Cross-site scripting is one of the most common techniques for hacking application layers and is known as CSS[6] or XSS. The attacker takes advantage of the vulnerabilities of the web application and sends malicious code to collect important personal details from the victim.

HOW CROSS-SITE SCRIPTING AFFECTS YOU

Normally, there are two types of web pages, one of them being static and the other dynamic. Both contain text and HTML code that the server generates and the client browser interprets. This is the way a website is visible to you through your computer browser. Static web pages are non-interactive and the server is able to exercise full control over how your browser will interpret the page. Dynamic pages, on the other hand, depend on the interaction of the user to display their content. In this case, the server has incomplete control over the code. Attackers use this incomplete control to introduce mistrusted content into the web page.

WHAT CAN AN ATTACKER DO WITH CSS?

The attacker can place a malicious Flash, HTML, ActiveX, VBScript or JavaScript code into the vulnerable dynamic web page. This fools the user, as the attacker executes the script on the user's machine, and gathers data from the user.

With this malicious CSS or XSS code, the attacker can compromise sensitive and private information, steal cookies or manipulate them and create valid looking requests.

HOW TO PREVENT CLICKJACKING AND CROSS-SITE SCRIPTING

One of the best methods recommended to prevent clickjacking is to use the latest browsers that have built-in protection against this form of attack. The latest versions of Firefox,

Chrome, IE and several others have this feature built-in, while there are plug-ins that do the work for others. In addition, all browser plug-ins must be updated to their latest version.

Apart from the browsers, clickjacking prevention also lies with the website and web application developers. They need to learn and write code to prevent clickjacking, using suggestions from the Code Secure Blog.

Similar diligence is required from programmers and necessary security testing must be done to prevent cross-site scripting. **The Acunetix Web Vulnerability Scanner can scan and tell you whether your website has vulnerability for XSS.**

REFERENCES:

1. Bachfeld, D., The H Security, *CSP: Thwarting cross-site scripting and click-jacking attacks.* Available from: <http://www.h-online.com/security/features/CSP-Thwarting-cross-site-scripting-and-click-jacking-attacks-1216438.html>. [29 March 2011].

2. OWASP, *Clickjacking.* Available from: <https://www.owasp.org/index.php/Clickjacking>. [3 April 2013].

3. O'Donnell, A., About.com Guide, *How to Protect Yourself From Clickjacking Attacks.* Available from: <http://netsecurity.about.com/od/antivirusandmalware/a/The-Dangers-Of-Clickjacking.htm>. [].

4. Acunetix, *Cross Site Scripting Attack.* Available from: <http://www.acunetix.com/websitesecurity/cross-site-scripting/>. [2013].

16 | BENEFITS OF APPLICATION SOFTWARE SECURITY

WHAT IS THE THREAT?

F laws in application software could cause vulnerability to remote compromise such as failing to sanitize user inputs, not checking properly the size of the user input and not initializing and/or clearing variables properly. To gain control over vulnerable machines running such software, attackers use various exploits such as SQL injection attacks; click jacking of code; buffer overflows; cross-site scripting; cross-site request forgery; and many others.

As an example of such an attack, in 2008, more than one million web-servers were turned into infection engines after being exploited using SQL injection. Using these servers, attackers compromised trusted websites from state governments and other organizations. Hundreds of thousands of visitors who accessed those websites had their browsers infected.

HOW DOES IT AFFECT THE ORGANIZATION?

Application software is usually unprotected for ease-of-deployment or ease-of-use as supplied by the manufacturers. . If left unaltered, it is easy for attackers to plant malware or a Trojan Horse to gain access to and take control of the network of the organization.

Unsecured application software can prove expensive to the organization. Theft by stealth of personal data such as credit card information alone costs the global economy upwards of $1 trillion a year. On average, individual businesses spend almost $3.8 million for countering, mitigating and cleaning up after a cyber-attack. An average customer loses up to $1,000 per attack from malware spread through unsecured application software. In addition, along with cybercrime, there is the fear and the loss of trust that customers usually feel for the compromised organizations.

Attackers use unsecured application software to plant malware, which is a broad umbrella term comprising spyware, Trojans, worms, viruses, bots and other such malicious programs. The consequences can range from the relatively harmless annoying pop-ups appearing in web browsers to extremely severe, such as identity and financial theft.

Attackers can take control of the entire network, once they are able to plant malware. Some malicious programs can replicate themselves and spread to other computers. Others can collect information without the user being aware and send it secretly to hackers who can then use it for further malicious purposes. Usernames and passwords can be recorded when users log into bank websites and can be used to gain access to accounts for stealing funds.

HOW CAN THIS THREAT BE MITIGATED?

Since malware comprises many types of malicious programs, no single solution exists to combat all the threats. For overall security, a holistic approach is the best practice. This involves deployment of different defenses for web security such as web application firewalls, intrusion detection systems, secure coding, firewalls and regular vulnerability assessments.

Application software must be hardened for security before deployment and periodically tested for vulnerabilities. Anti-malware scanning is a new tool that is an effective supplement to the traditional scanners.

These tools usually maintain a database to keep track of the latest malware threats. Other best practices include dynamic updates and timely removal of site seals.

REFERENCES:

1. The SANS Institute, *Critical Control 6: Application Software Security*. Available from: <http://www.sans.org/critical-security-controls/control.php?id=6>. [2013].

2. Symantec, *WHITE PAPER: THE ONGOING MALWARE THREAT*. Available from: <http://www.geotrust.com/anti-malware-scan/malware-threat-white-paper.pdf>. [2012].

3. Hau, D., The SANS Institute, *Unauthorized Access – Threats, Risk, and Control*. Available from: <http://www.giac.org/paper/gsec/3161/unauthorized-access-threats-risk-control/105264>. [11 July 2003].

17 | HOW DOES NETWORK AUTOMATION BRING NETWORKING AND SECURITY TOGETHER?

WHAT IS NETWORK AUTOMATION?

With network automation, an organization improves the availability of its network services. The phrase fundamentally describes the processes, methods, and technologies used in enterprises and large organizations to configure and manage their network devices such as the hubs, routers and switches.

In the past decade, there has been an explosion of increasingly complex network devices. In addition, with the adoption of BYOD policies, cloud services, virtualization, and mobile working practices, the challenges faced by the modern network has increased exponentially. .

An example would be in order here. Only a few years ago, one needed to punch a hole in the single firewall to let a new service request through. Today, the same request requires a change in several layers of security, changes in ACL rules and in multiple firewalls, switches and integrated routers. The introduction of multiple vendors further complicates the issue.

Classically, in an enterprise, the security teams are responsible for the firewalls and the network teams are responsible for the routers and switches. The roles of the two teams have always been clearly defined. However, with the networks becoming larger, broader, and more complex, both the teams have to work more closely and collaborate.

THE PROBLEMS IN BRINGING NETWORKING AND SECURITY TOGETHER

Although collaboration is beneficial, there is a downside to it. The security and the networking teams have specified experience and knowledge in their own domains. They are unlikely to be able to carry out the tasks required by the other team, and this may involve a significant risk of creating errors.

For example, members of the networking team are not likely to be familiar with the different nuances and subtleties of syntax used by various vendors. Likewise, the security teams are more adept at setting internal policies governing the best practices of the enterprise, and this can impact the networking team.

If one team does not have the expertise to perform the tasks of the other team, frustrations and challenges can quickly grow and affect the overall functioning of the enterprise.

HOW DOES NETWORK AUTOMATION HELP?

With automation, a high volume of required changes can be analyzed by the security team, tested, and provisioned across the network, saving considerable amount of time. Automation takes care of the different rules and syntax required for separate devices and vendors, which is the major consumer of time in such cases.

With automation, network teams are able to make changes in firewall policies as required in one place and distribute these changes across the network quickly, with automation taking care of the multi-vendor devices. This reduces the time and effort required for the deployment, and eliminates the need to make changes to individual devices.

HOW DOES NETWORK AUTOMATION INCREASE EF-FICIENCY?

Network automation provides a holistic, automated approach over the entire network management. It extends over the domain of fault, performance, availability, configuration, change, compliance, and process automation. The key benefits can be listed as:

- Cost reduction by automating manual compliance and configuration tasks;

- Audit and compliance requirements pass easily with audit and compliance reports and proactive policy deployments;

- Improvement in network security by the recognition and fixing of vulnerabilities before they impact the network;

- Increase in network uptime and availability by preventing mis-configurations and inconsistencies;

- Application integrations are delivered by process-powered automation, delivering full IT lifecycle workflow automation.

REFERENCES:

1. Search Networking, *Network automation tools: Should you build or buy?* Available from: <http://searchnetworking.techtarget.com/Network-automation-tools-Should-you-build-or-buy>. [Oct 2013].

2. Pao, P., Hewlett Packard, *Efficient change, automated configuration & secure compliance.* Available from: <http://www8.hp.com/us/en/software-solutions/software.html?compURI=1169982#.Ud6GzeEu18M>. [2013].

3. Nye, S., Help Net Security, *Bringing networking and security together through network automation.* Available from: <http://www.net-security.org/article.php?id=1837>. [10 May 2013].

18 | THE COLLATERAL DAMAGE OF PHPSESSID ATTACKS

WHAT IS A BRUTEFORCE OF PHPSESSID ATTACK?

Many websites offer to keep you logged in ("remember me on this website") after you have logged in. This may be convenient in that you do not have to log in repeatedly if you are visiting the site frequently. However, for an attacker on the prowl, you become an easy target as an attacker can go into the website masquerading as you. In technical jargon, the way the attacker learns both your username and passwords and can then impersonate you is Bruteforce of PHPSESSID or session fixation.

WHAT HAPPENS DURING THE ATTACK?

During session fixation, an attacker snooping around can get a valid session ID from an application. The attacker then forces the application to use the same session ID. He usually does this by sending the victim a link to a website with the session ID attached to the URL. Once the victim uses the link, the attacker uses the information to guess the username and password of the user, and the website the user was visiting. It is then easy for the attacker to impersonate the user.

On the server side, the PHP framework issues a session token when a client session is started. The token comprises a lot of information such as the IP address of the client, current time in seconds and microseconds, a combined PHP lcg sample and optionally additional information (entropy) from available sources.

Even though the PHP string is a big string and MD5 encrypted, the session ID string follows a definite pattern, with parameters such as the IP address and the PHP_combined_lcq at specific places. To generate the actual values by guessing them would take a lot of effort by ordinary means and this is where the brute force technology comes in. The attacker systematically tries every possible combination of symbols, letters and numbers until he discovers the one correct combination that works.

However, depending on the length of the password used, the number of permutations and combinations could be extremely huge to be of practical use and it may take the attacker years to find one password. Attackers therefore use dictionary words, wordlists and smart rulesets to start with, and this could put all accounts at risk by flooding your site with unnecessary traffic.

WHAT IS THE HARM CAUSED BY SUCH ATTACKS?

An attacker trying to guess username and passwords may send a huge number of requests to the server, flooding the server with traffic and causing a denial of service to the authentic users.

Once he gains entry into a vulnerable user account, not only can the attacker steal sensitive information from the account, he can also plant malware that may compromise other accounts as well.

Using the compromised server, the attacker can turn it into a zombie and attach it to his botnet to create further attacks that are more powerful.

HOW CAN SUCH ATTACKS BE PREVENTED?

Usually some very effective mechanisms are used to prevent such attacks. One is to login the user only from a certain IP address. If there is a change in the IP address during a login session, another level of authentication of secret questions is used to identify if the user is genuine. Therefore, even if the attacker has managed to guess the username and password by the brute force method, there is another deterrent to gain access.

Other effective methods used are:

- Assigning unique login URLs to a section of the users in blocks

- Preventing automatic attacks by using CAPTCHA

- Place the attacked account in a lockdown mode with limited capabilities

- Combinations of the above.

REFERENCES:

1. Susser, B., *Not So Random Numbers. Take Two- The Brute-force pf PHPSESSID.* Avaliable from: <http://bot24. blogspot.in/2012/09/not-so-random-numbers-take-two.html>. [6 September 2012].

2. ZZO The Researcher, *PHPSESSID information leakage.* Avaliable from: <http://dev-zzo.net/blog/2013/04/ phpsessid-information-leakage/>. [6 April 2013].

3. Burnett, M., System Administration Database, *Blocking Brute Force Attacks.* Avaliable from: <http://www. cs.virginia.edu/~csadmin/gen_support/brute_force. php>. [2007].

19

HOW TO DETECT AND DEFEND AGAINST SOPHISTICATED MALWARE WITH DOMAIN NAME SYSTEM (DNS) ANOMALY

WHAT IS A DNS ANOMALY?

To prevent the takedown of a botnet, cybercriminals are using increasingly sophisticated methods of communication. One of them is DGA or Domain Generation Algorithms, and these are designed to evade detection with increase in web traffic. They do this by malwares using the DGA to generate domain names, which bots use as rendezvous points with their bot controllers. If the controller is offline, these domain names are used to restore communication between them.

Domain Name Services or DNS being an essential component for the Internet to function, cybercriminals cannot get around without using DNS. However, since their nefarious activities are atypical of normal DNS usage, this is an anomaly, which can be used for the detection of their activity.

WHAT HAPPENS DURING A DNS ANOMALY?

Normally, when there is a request for a specific domain name, the DNS server will translate it into an IP address. If successful, the request will create HTTP traffic towards that domain. However, if a domain is entered incorrectly, the request falls through and the DNS server generates an NX-DOMAIN response.

In the case of malicious DNS traffic, the sequence followed is different. The infecting malware makes a huge number of simultaneous requests for a domain, as it has to guess to locate the correct domain of its cybercriminal master. Essentially, the malware has a predetermined list of its masters, and by searching, connects to the active one. However, this process leads to large amounts of NXDOMAIN responses causing a high level of detectable noise, which easily flags the presence of the malware threat.

To avoid detection, malware using the DGA communicates with new domains only intermittently, which frustrates the efforts of detection. This method of detection uses traffic analysis, which requires generation of static timing. Malware avoids this with its random nature of communication. This method of agile DNS generation helps the malware evade blacklists. Therefore, the methods of detecting malware by comparing them against blacklists are no more effective than in the past.

This makes the task of monitoring DNS traffic even more complicated. In normal conditions, about 12 NXDOMAINS are generated by DNS traffic every hour. Some malicious infections have been known to generate more than 400 NXDOMAINs per hour.

WHAT CAN BE DETECTED BY MONITORING A DNS ANOMALY?

In view of the evasive tactics malware are now adopting, sophisticated and comprehensive systems are necessary to collect DNS traffic by capturing it through monitoring sensors.

By monitoring DNS traffic, malware infection can be detected. However, an analysis of the data is necessary to reveal the malware source of the infected host.

HOW TO DETECT AND LOCATE DNS ANOMALIES

Software such as Passive DNS helps to aggregate duplicate traffic, while keeping the logs small. The analysis tool looks for specific methods to search through the NXDOMAIN logs for:

- Domain length – mainly broken up into 6 different length categories;
- Character makeup – Consonants only, characters only and alphanumeric only;
- Top Level Domains – 272 variations of TLD.

REFERENCES:

1. Weymes, B., Data Net Security, *DNS anomaly detection: Defend against sophisticated malware.* Available from: <http://www.net-security.org/article.php?id=1844>. [28 May 2013].

2. Hall, S., ISC Diary, *Cyber Intelligence Tsunami.* Available from: <https://isc.sans.edu/diary/A+Poor+Man %27s+DNS+Anomaly+Detection+Script/13918>. [July 2013].

3. Narang, R., INFOSEC Institute, *Traffic Anomaly Detection – TCP and DNS.* Available from: <http://resources. infosecinstitute.com/traffic-anomaly-detection/>. [1 June 2012].

20 | IS HTTP ENOUGH TO PROTECT YOUR COOKIES FROM XSS VULNERABILITIES?

WHAT ARE XSS VULNERABILITIES?

Cross Site Scripting or XSS happens when an attacker presents you with a malicious website looking like its original, and asks you to fill in your credentials. When your browser sends the cookies over to the malicious website, the attacker decodes your information.

WHAT HAPPENS DURING AN XSS ATTACK?

Although Cross Site Scripting is one of the most common forms of attack, most people underestimate its power to exploit. In an XSS attack, the attacker targets the scripts executed on the client-side rather than on the server-side. Mostly the Internet security vulnerabilities of the client-side is responsible, because of JavaScript, HTML, VBScript, ActiveX and Flash scripting languages, which are the major culprits for these kinds of exploits.

In an XSS attack, the attacker achieves their goal by manipulating the client-side scripts of the user's web application. With such a manipulation, he can embed a script within a page such that it executes each time the page is loaded or whenever a certain associated event is performed.

In another variation of the XSS attack, the attacker infects a legitimate web page with his malicious client-side script. When the user opens the web page in his browser, the script downloads itself and from then on, executes whenever the user opens that specific page.

As an example of an XSS attack, a malicious user injects his script into a legitimate shopping site URL. This URL redirects a genuine user to an identical but fake site. The page on the fake site runs a script to capture the cookie of the genuine user who has landed on the page. Using the cookie the malicious user now hijacks the genuine user's session.

Most site owners do not realize the gravity of XSS attacks, which steal sensitive data from back-end databases. However, the consequences of an XSS attack against a web application can be quite damaging as both application functionality and daily business operation may be seriously compromised.

If an enterprise's site is vulnerable to XSS exploits, present and future customers may fear leakage of sensitive information and discontinue their business association. The loss of trust will definitely not bode well for the future of the enterprise. It might also lead to a defaced application and a public embarrassment for the enterprise, much to the delight of the attacker.

Exploitation through XSS may lead to the following:

- Theft of identity;
- Access to restricted or sensitive information;

- Free access to otherwise paid for content;
- Spying on the habits of the user;
- Changing the functionality of the browser;
- Public defamation of an enterprise or an individual;
- Defacement of a web application;
- Denial of Service to genuine users.

In several cases of XSS attacks, malicious users have made use of security flaws in high-profile web sites and obtained user information and credit card details to carry out expensive transactions. Legitimate users were duped into visiting a legitimate-looking page, which then captured their credentials and sent the details to the attacker.

Although the above incidents may not be as bad as attackers gaining access to an enterprise database, customers easily lose faith in the application's security. For the owner of the vulnerable web site, such incidents can easily turn into legal nightmares, liabilities and quite possibly loss of business.

SHOULD YOU WAIT FOR YOUR SITE TO BE ATTACKED?

Carry out necessary security testing of your site regularly and have your programmers learn to be diligent about such threats.

Enable key security controls of the web application such as cookie handling, framing and processing of JavaScript, which dictate security properties to the web browser.

Use HTTPOnly to minimize the impact of XSS vulnerability by preventing JavaScript access to the session cookie.

REFERENCES:

1. Atwood, J., Coding Horror, *Protecting Your Cookies: HttpOnly*. Availale from: <http://www.codinghorror.com/blog/2008/08/protecting-your-cookies-httponly.html>. [28 August 2008].

2. Melton, J., White Hat Security, *Session Cookie HttpOnly Flag Java*. Availale from: <https://blog.whitehatsec.com/session-cookie-httponly-flag-java/#.Uc0Ef-hUt11w>. [17 May 2012].

3. Coates, M., Security For The Web, *Enabling Browser Security in Web Applications*. Available from: <http://michael-coates.blogspot.in/2011/03/enabling-browser-security-in-web.html>. [31 March 2011].

4. Guillaumier, J., Acunetix, *Cross Site Scripting – XSS – The Underestimated Exploit*. Available from: <http://www.acunetix.com/websitesecurity/xss/>. [?].

21 | SECURITY CONCERNS OF BYOD IN LARGE ORGANIZATIONS

WHAT IS BYOD AND WHY IS IT IMPORTANT?

Many organizations today allow their employees to use their own mobile devices at work. You are allowed to Bring Your Own Device (BYOD) to work, as it answers many problems. However, this raises several complex security issues.

Instead of struggling to provide all employees with the latest technologies, the common practice now is to allow employees to use their own device at work. This naturally increases the risks to the existing network of the organization. A study by the Ponemon Institute found 81% of healthcare organizations permit their employees to BYOD and connect to the organization's network. However, more than 54% of the respondents were not confident of the security of these personally owned devices.

WHAT ARE THE CHALLENGES OF BYOD?

It is most critical that enterprises decide, for mobile device access, what data and systems will be accessible to BYOD employees, as well as determining the level of access. Another issue they would have to consider is monitoring employee emails for the type of content and attachments using suitable software.

In specific terms, the challenges may include:

- Accessibility to systems and data;

- Employee access and usage;

- Type of device and its operating system;

- Device security

A risk assessment of enterprise data and systems exposure is advised with regard to mobile devices. In some cases, assessment may also have to cover the risk of loss.

Not all employees need access to the enterprise system and data. Only those whose job function necessitates access to the company's data and systems must be allowed access via a mobile device.

It may be cumbersome for the enterprise to try to provide support to a number of different devices, given the multitude of operating systems and wide variety of mobile devices. Enterprises may reduce the expenses involved by limiting BYOD to a few types.

When securing a device, it may mean installation of additional apps for enhancement of password security, anti-virus and anti-malware. The built-in mobile capabilities for password do not meet current corporate standards. Therefore, for enhanced security, it may be necessary to identify and select required applications for the devices.

Although updates to device technology and operating systems are issued frequently, they require evaluating and validating before deployment. This is another challenge to owners of enterprises as the employees most often control the devices and their updates.

WHAT SORT OF POLICIES WOULD BE GOOD FOR BYOD?

The first requirement for effectively controlling mobile devices as with all other IT services is a comprehensive and company-wide set of policies and guidelines. The next requirement is training all employees to enable them to understand the risks involved with the convenience and privileges of being allowed to use mobile devices.

For securing BYODs, some of the important security measures all devices must incorporate include:

- Strong passcodes;
- Data loss prevention (DLP) and anti-virus protection;
- Encryption for internal storage, removable media and cloud storage;
- Mobile Device Management (MDM) to wipe data off when lost or stolen;
- Application control.

REFERENCES:

1. Zorz, M., Data Net Security, *BYOD: The why and the how*. Available from: <http://www.net-security.org/article. php?id=1853>. [21 June 2013].

2. Sophos Solutions, *BYOD Risks & Rewards*. Available from: <http://www.sophos.com/en-us/security-news-trends/security-trends/byod-risks-rewards/how-to-secure-byods.aspx>. [?].

3. Cisco, *BYOD Smart Solution*. Available from: <http://www.cisco.com/web/solutions/trends/byod_smart_solution/index.html>. [?].

22 | CONTROLLING ADMINISTRATIVE PRIVILEGES

WHAT HAPPENS IF ADMINISTRATIVE PRIVILEGES ARE NOT UNDER CONTROL?

One of the primary ways for an attacker to gain entry into an enterprise network is by misusing the administrative privileges. Attackers usually follow one of two methods for gaining access. In the first method, the attacker manages to fool one of the privileged users of a workstation into opening a document from a malicious website, or surf a website hosting malicious content, which automatically exploits the visitor's browser.

The malicious code then runs on the victim's computer, and if the victim user's account has administrative privileges, takes over their computer completely. After this it is relatively simple for the attacker to install sniffers, keystroke loggers, and various remote control software to then dig out administrative passwords thus gaining access to sensitive data. Such attacks are common through e-mails. If an unsuspecting administrator were to open an e-mail containing an infected attachment, the attacker gains access to the system using this as a pivot point to attack other systems.

Attackers may also gain access by a secondary method: guessing or cracking a password used by an administrator. This gives the attacker access to the target machine.

With administrative privileges distributed widely and loosely, the attacker's work of compromising these privileges is made easier since so many other accounts are now available.

HOW DOES THIS AFFECT THE ENTERPRISE?

An administrator has absolute privileges over the entire enterprise network. If the attacker were able to elevate his privileges equal to the level of an administrator, then he could masquerade as the administrator himself and quickly gain control over all the resources in the network.

This allows the attacker to inflict major damage to the enterprise by stealing or modifying confidential data, disrupting daily operating procedures, upsetting financial transactions, slowing down network traffic, denying legitimate service to other users and diverting communication and sensitive data to offsite malicious servers.

WHAT IS THE BEST WAY TO MITIGATE THIS THREAT?

Use administrative privileges only when necessary. Introduce focused auditing on all persons who use the administrative privileges and monitor all anomalous behavior.

Inventory all the administrative privileges using an automated tool, and validate that a senior executive has authorized each person who uses administrative privileges.

Change over all administrative passwords to be complex formations of intermixed special characters, numbers, letters and alphabets. Strong passwords of sufficient length make it difficult for the attacker to guess and to crack.

Passwords for administrators should be changed at frequent intervals. Any new device, when being introduced to the networked environment, must have all its default passwords changed to longer and relatively more difficult passwords.

Passwords for all systems must be stored in an encrypted format, only readable by those with super-user privileges. The control lists must ensure that administrative accounts are used only for activities requiring system administration and not for general activities such as reading e-mails.

REFERENCES:

1. The SANS Institute, *Critical Control 12: Controlled Use of Administrative Privileges.* Available from: <http://www.sans.org/critical-security-controls/control.php?id=12>. [2013].

2. Hau, D., The SANS Institute, *Unauthorized Access – Threats, Risk, and Control.* Available from: <http://www.giac.org/paper/gsec/3161/unauthorized-access-threats-risk-control/105264>. [11 July 2013].

3. Computer Economica, *Security Threats in Employee Misuse of IT Resources.* Available from: <http://www.computereconomics.com/article.cfm?id=1436>. [March 2009].

23 | USER REPORTING TO STRENGTHEN YOUR SECURITY

WHAT IS USER REPORTING?

Similar to cyber criminals targeting and using employees to cast their nefarious activities on organizations through social engineering, enterprises can make user reporting a strong and potent weapon against cyber-attacks.

A huge opportunity exists within the organization to collect vital information about threats from both outside as well as inside the organization. By developing a formal process, employees can report suspicious behavior such as emails and provide real-time information on threats. This formal process also allows for an improved response along with fast mitigation activities.

Criminals use phishing as an online fraud technique to entice users into disclosing their personal information. Usually they use tempting emails, threats and mimics of well-known web sites to get to the user's credentials and steal personal finance information. If the attacker is able to penetrate the enterprise network, the organization can lose valuable intellectual property.

WHAT ARE THE BENEFITS OF ACTIVE USER REPORTING?

Instead of adding a few software programs to watch over the activities on the corporate network, trained employees can act as an army of sensors and do the job many times better.

As an example, the receipt of a suspicious email, when reported to the administrator can trigger a reactive response controlling the removal of similar emails from the mailboxes of other users. Blocking outbound traffic and redirecting and capturing traffic for analysis can thus immediately control the damage.

HOW SHOULD ACTIVE USER REPORTING BE STARTED WITHIN THE ENTERPRISE?

Many security administrators are of the opinion that users cannot be a source of useful information. However, they miss the fact that people must be trained to understand what they should be looking for, to recognize typical signs of phishing in emails and must have a simple process for reporting. The enterprise can thus turn their employees into a solid wall of defense that will be more effective than the technology employed.

User reporting must be a part of the organization's culture. The employees have to be made aware of the important role they play toward the security of the organization. The IT employees must value the information they receive from users. The organization can take several steps to encourage employees to report suspicious behavior.

The process of reporting must remain simple. Since reporting suspicious activity is beyond the job description of an employee, this should be made as simple as possible, rather than a burden. All suspicious activity must be reported to one single address and that address must be well known to all employees.

Employees must be made aware of why they are reporting and how their reporting is beneficial to their organization. There must be no fear of job loss if, for example an employee inadvertently clicked on a suspicious link. This aspect is crucial, as no one is likely to report if there is a fear of negative consequences.

Response to each reporting must be visible and immediate. Active security enforces a psychological repercussion that encourages further reporting.

REFERENCES:

1. Higbee, A., The Data Chain, *Training your Staff to Stop Phishing Attacks*. Available from: <http://www.thedata-chain.com/articles/2013/5/training_your_staff_to_stop_phishing_attacks?contentpartner=cloud_computing_congress>. [29 May 2013].

2. Microsoft, *Identify fraudulent e-mail and phishing schemes*. Available from: <http://office.microsoft.com/en-001/outlook-help/identify-fraudulent-e-mail-and-phishing-schemes-HA001140002.aspx>. [2013].

3. Greaux, S., Help Net Security, *Human sensors: How encouraging user reporting strengthens security*. Available from: <http://www.net-security.org/article.php?id=1839>. [14 May 2013].

24 | OVERLOOKED THREATS FROM INSIDERS OR FROM DATA EXFILTRATION

WHAT IS DATA EXFILTRATION?

Data exfiltration is the removing or sending of data out of the enterprise without due authorization.

Technology allows employees to do their jobs efficiently at the workplace and fulfill the mission of their organization. However, malicious insiders can cause harm to the organization using these same technologies. Usually Information Technology support teams and Information Security implement physical protection for workstations, servers and mobile devices and have Access Control Lists for restricting access to data. Other devices, such as papers, printers, scanners, fax machines, and copiers may be overlooked and remain with little or no protection.

Malicious insiders may use these technologies to extract sensitive company documents and remove the information from the company to start their own business or to share with competitors for potential gains.

117

While e-mailing sensitive documents may leave an electronic trail and lead to subsequent prosecution, printing on paper does not leave any evidence once the paper exits the premises of the organization. Research organizations, design departments and other sensitive areas are especially vulnerable. Commercial activities are also at risk, where trade secrets may be printed and thereby stolen.

Information not in digital form is more difficult to print on paper, but a scanner can make that work easier. It can convert information residing on paper to digital form, which becomes easier to print or send electronically.

Although fax machines are now outdated, they can be used to transmit information very easily such that the act can be almost impossible to detect. Often an insider can send information out of the organization undetected, using the fax machine.

Insiders often use copiers to duplicate information in an organization. This allows them to send the information out of the enterprise without removing the original documents, which could have led to early detection.

HOW DOES DATA EXFILTRATION AFFECT ENTERPRISES?

An insider attack and subsequent data exfiltration may be extremely harmful to the enterprise, depending on the type of data taken out. A parent company lost nearly $3 million in one case of research documents being handed over to a competitor component manufacturer. In another case, trade secrets and physical blueprints were sold, causing a loss of $150 million. A telecommunications company lost nearly $1.5 million, because their trade secret documents were physically scanned converting them into digital form, and subsequently posted on a hacking website. When a disgruntled engineer sent technical drawings from his parent company to a competitor organization via fax and e-mails, he caused a loss of $1.5 million.

HOW TO MITIGATE THE RISK OF DATA EXFILTRATION BY INSIDERS

- Incorporate all devices into the enterprise risk assessment and use policies to govern their use;

- Use central logging to store and index insider behavior on networks;

- Track user identity and suspicious behavior with software to identify malware and use of exploits.

Printer activity is something that all organizations must monitor carefully and retain logs of documents printed. The organization must audit the logs as part of their log-monitoring program. Any anomalies such as printing before or after business hours or any user printing an unusually high number of documents must trigger an alert.

Enterprises must provide authorized access to scanners and only a user with proper authorization should be able to scan a document that is not in a digital form already. Printed documents must be provided commensurate levels of protection to that of digital files. People who receive printouts must have the required permissions to have access to these hard copies.

Employees must have limited access to fax machines and copiers. A trusted employee must review and transmit the document, after logging the details of the document and the transmission.

Central log storage and indexing can be used to detect malicious insider behavior on the enterprise network. Splunk is one such log storage and indexing engine. For tracking user identity and suspicious behavior, many organizations are using software such as StealthWatch.

REFERENCES:

1. Software Engineering Institute, Carnegie Mellon University, *Data Exfiltration and Output Devices - An Overlooked Threat.* Available from: <http://www.cert.org/blogs/insider_threat/2011/10/data_exfiltration_and_output_devices_-_an_overlooked_threat.html>. [17 October, 2011].

2. Montelibano, J. & Hanley, M., Software Engineering Institute, Carnegie Mellon University, *Insider Threat Control: Using Centralized Logging to Detect Data Exfiltration Near Insider Termination.* Available from: <http://www.sei.cmu.edu/library/abstracts/reports/11tn024.cfm>. [October 2011].

3. Lncope, *Thwarting Insider Threats with StealthWatch.* Available from: <http://www.lancope.com/solutions/security-threats/insider-threats/>. [2013].

25 | ONLINE FRAUD AND MONEY MULE RISKS

On the Internet, there are plenty of job vacancies for a 'Money Transfer Agent'. People also receive emails asking for help to transfer huge quantities of money from one country to another. The overabundance makes one wonder about the genuine nature of these offers, and causes many job seekers to be suspicious.

WHAT ARE ON-LINE FRAUDS AND MONEY MULES?

The sad fact is most of these online job offers are frauds and could lead to an inadvertent criminal record. It could also lead to an exclusion from the banking system for the naive job seeker who is drawn to such illegal activities.

The online job seeker is often used as an unwitting 'money mule' and led to misusing their bank account by laundering money through their account. In 2012, the second most identified fraud was through misuse of bank accounts. More than 45,000 confirmed instances of such fraud were identified and several of them bore the hallmark of such 'money mule' activity.

Usually fraudsters use the money from illegal activities such as fake lotteries, boiler room frauds, drug dealing and investments, prostitution and people trafficking in such frauds. They try to push 'dirty money' through in an effort to make it appear 'clean'. Legally, accounts that are utilized to launder money must be closed and international regulators fine them heavily for failure to do so.

THE RISKS PEOPLE FACE FROM ONLINE FRAUDS AND MONEY MULES

You are at a risk of becoming a victim of online fraud, should you lose your personal information to others. You and your family may face threats and be forced to perform online fraud. Different types of online frauds are:

- Phishing – Fraud websites decked up to masquerade as genuine sites to steal usernames, passwords and banking information.

- Money Mules – Lucrative fraudulent jobs offered to young adults and teens luring them into money laundering activities.

- Online Bank Fraud – Numerous people bank online considering the convenience. Online banking poses security risks involving Worms, Trojan Horses, imposter websites and fake e-mails, threatening to steal your credentials with each online transaction and purchase.

HOW DO MONEY MULES WORK?

Fraudsters usually contact their prospective victims or money mules with advertisements for jobs via job search websites, Internet chat rooms or spam e-mails. They advertise the jobs as financial management work, adding that special knowledge for the job is unnecessary. Some fraudsters may also ask the mules to sign some official looking employment contracts.

Mules, once recruited, will receive funds into their accounts, most of them stolen from other compromised accounts. Mules will then be asked to take out the funds and forward them to overseas accounts typically using wire transfer services. For their services, they will receive a commission payment.

With their account being involved in the money laundering transaction, the mule also becomes an unwitting participant in the frauds.

HOW TO PROTECT YOURSELF FROM MONEY MULE FRAUDS

Carefully inspect any unsolicited opportunity or offer to make easy money before you part with your personal information. Most of the frauds will be from overseas companies and it will be difficult for you to find out if they are authentic.

People phishing for information may replicate the website of a genuine company to entice you into their folds. They may even register a similar looking web address that adds authenticity to the fraud. However, there will be subtle differences in the website URLs and web addresses and you must be extremely careful and alert to be able to detect the differences.

One simple way to ascertain the genuineness of such offers is to call the company who has purportedly placed the ads. By searching for and visiting the home page of the company, you will be able to find out their contact details. Contact them with reference to the advertisement and you will immediately know if they are genuinely recruiting people.

REFERENCES:

1. CIFAS, *Beware Job Ads for Money Transfer Agents warns CIFAS.* Available from: <http://www.cifas.org.uk/moneymulescams_feb>. [26 February 2013].

2. ICICI Bank, *Money Mule.* Available from: <http://www.icicibank.com/online-safe-banking/beware-of-fraud/money-mule.html>. [2013].

3. eBay, *What Risks Do You Face From Online Fraud? Money Mules.* Available from: <http://www.ebay.co.uk/gds/What-Risks-Do-You-Face-From-Online-Fraud-Money-Mules/10000000006003964/g.html>. [2013].

26 | CLOUD COMPUTING THREATS

WHAT THREATS ARE FACED BY CLOUD COMPUTING?

Compared with incidences of computer security that affect corporate systems in general, cloud service providers have faced relatively fewer attacks. This could be because the providers of cloud services have stronger security, as they are more concerned about the data breach and the reputational consequences that would ensue. In the world of cloud computing, threats could be faced at three levels – the service provider, the tenant or the user of the service, and the transmission path connecting the two.

Some of the security and crime risks that the providers of cloud services face are as follows:

- Authentication issues

- Denial of service attacks

- Use of cloud computing for criminal activities

- Illegal activities by the service provider

- Attacks on physical security

- Insider abuse of access

- Malware

- Cross-guest virtual machine breaches or side channel attacks

- Insecure or obsolete encryption

- Structured Query Language injection

Tenants of cloud computing may face security and crime risks of the following nature:

- Phishing

- Domain name system attacks

- Compromising of the device accessing the cloud

- Access management issues

Some attacks that target the transmission of data could be of the following nature:

- Session hijacking and session riding

- Man-in-the-middle attacks

- Network/packet sniffing

When username and password combinations are obtained and used without authorization, it may lead to authentication issues on cloud systems. The information may have been obtained by various means, including guessing, key-logging malware, password recovery mechanisms or social engineering attacks.

Attackers can send a flood of traffic to overwhelm the websites, making them inaccessible to legitimate users. This type of denial of service is generally perpetrated using a botnet and causes widespread distributed denial of service or DDoS.

As the cloud services are meant for sharing resources, existing accounts may be compromised or new accounts may be created using stolen credit card details and credentials. This reduces the cost to the offenders, and makes it difficult to trace the source of the attack, especially when jurisdictions are crossed.

Providers of cloud services may themselves be involved in illegal activities such as piracy. When authorities close the services, all other users of the service suffer, as they are unable to access their documents.

Attackers are also known to have physically attacked the providers of cloud services, stealing hardware, and accessing servers without proper authorization causing loss of data.

Discontented employees of a cloud service provider are easy prey to attackers and may misuse their privileges to obtain access to stored data or disrupt access to legitimate users in lieu of potential perceived gains. More than 50% of the ICT[7] professionals were concerned about insider threats in the cloud, including planting malware.

If the victim's and the attacker's virtual machines are both located on the same physical machine, there could be side channel attack. The attacker may access the data of the other tenants using the same physical resources.

Insecure or obsolete encryption may be another opportunity for attackers to read unauthorized data. Analyzing accessed positions and monitoring the query access pattern of the client may also lead to reading sensitive information.

Attackers may inject Structured Query Language code that performs erroneously in the database back end. This could lead to data access and possible modification without due authorization.

Phishing and DNS attacks are other threats that users of cloud services face. These may not be linked directly to the cloud service itself, but the user may be hijacked to use another resource masquerading as the authentic one and made to disgorge all his credentials.

PREVENTIVE MEASURES

According to the CSA or the Cloud Security Alliance, there is no single-shot solution to preventing or reducing the risk of threats to the security of cloud computing. Their recommendations include a defensive and in-depth strategy, which includes security enforcements for computing, storage, network, application and the user, as well as monitoring.

REFERENCES:

1. Gonsalves, A., ReadWrite, *The 9 Top Threats Facing Cloud Computing*. Available from: <http://readwrite. com/2013/03/04/9-top-threats-from-cloud-computin g#awesm=~o8TDlRF1BuaCmO>. [4 March 2013].

2. Samson, T., InfoWorld, *9 top threats to cloud computing security*. Available from: <http://www.infoworld.com/t/ cloud-security/9-top-threats-cloud-computing-securi-ty-213428>. [25 February 2013].

3. Hutchings, A., Smith, R.G. & JamesL., Australian Institute of Criminology, *Cloud computing for small business: Criminal and security threats and prevention measures.* Available from: <http://www.aic.gov.au/publications/cur-rent%20series/tandi/441-460/tandi456.html>.   [May 2013].

27 | HOW TO PROTECT AGAINST WEB ATTACKS

I t is extremely difficult for a company, after noticing some unusual financial transactions, to immediately ascertain whether it was an internal fraud or embezzlement or a cyber-crime attack. Attacking a company from the outside and siphoning off funds through, say, fraudulent payroll accounts, is a common form of web attack. Between 2008 and 2010, attackers caused damages worth $3 million in at least 53 Seattle based enterprises, and this is just the tip of the iceberg.

NEVER BE COMPLACENT ABOUT SECURITY

Most companies think their system will hold against cyber-crime, and this complacency leads to their undoing when they find smart and ambitious crooks have breached their security. Careless disposal of old equipment such as old laptops, without proper data wipe-off, is also one of the many ways crooks can gain access to security systems.

Apart from the financial loss and the cost of repairs, being a victim of cyber-crime can cost a business its customers. Tabulus Inc. found in a survey that more than 80% of their respondents preferred to warn others to stop business deals with companies that had suffered a security breach. The survey also found that the same respondents held companies to be more trustworthy if these companies had no history of a security breach.

VULNERABLE WI-FI NETWORKS

Victims of cyber-attack are usually compromised via their unprotected Wi-Fi networks. Attacker gangs outfit their cars with high-powered antennas and drive around, scanning for poorly protected or unlocked networks. Once such a network is found, it is an easy task for the attackers to scour the machines on the network and steal passwords and financial data.

The best possible defense that a company can have against such exploits is to avoid wireless networks and use only wired networks. Wired networks are somewhat more secure because they need a physical connection to access them. If a wireless network is necessary, the service set identifier or SSID broadcasting function must be disabled on the wireless router. This prevents casual Wi-Fi snoops from discovering the now hidden network, as users who know the exact network name can only detect this. For added security, the network's information can be periodically changed and only the genuine users informed of the current network name and passcode.

Many Wi-Fi modems and routers still use the WEP encryption algorithm that is outdated by almost 10 years and is easily cracked by the attackers. This must be updated to the current standard WPA2, which is more difficult to break into.

E-MAILS AND HARMFUL WEBSITES

Attacks from spam e-mails and harmful websites push a lot of malware, Trojans, and viruses toward computers on the network, independent of whether the enterprise is using a wireless or a wired network. If the attack is successful, the malware generally installs malicious code that runs in the background, capturing login information and keystrokes to relay it to the attackers.

Anytime someone visits a site requiring a login and a password such as Facebook, bank, payroll, or whatever, the malware harvests the information and sends it to the attacker. With this information, the attacker masquerades as the original user and does his evil activities.

Installing anti-malware and anti-virus protection on both non-mobile as well as mobile devices can ensure that such attacks do not take effect. To be more secure, these protection software programs must be run after every software install. In addition, keeping all programs and hardware up to date is a necessary step against e-mail phishing and spoofing.

EMPLOYEE EDUCATION IS NECESSARY

It pays to educate all employees of the organization to look out for attacks and to recognize one when they see it. It must start with a company-wide internet policy, letting employees know what acceptable and prohibited on-line activities are allowed in the company.

REFERENCES:

1. Sarna, S., Small Business Digest, *Simple Steps Businesses Can Take to Protect Themselves from Cyber Crime*. Available from: <http://www.2sbdigest.com/Protect-Themselves-from-Cyber-Crime>. [2013].

2. Lemos, R., Dark Reading, *10 Web Threats That Could Harm Your Business*. Available from: <http://www.darkreading.com/vulnerability/10-web-threats-that-could-harm-your-busi/240150315>. [15 March 2013].

3. Pullen, J.P., Enterprenuer, *How to Protect Your Small Business Against a Cyber Attack*. Available from: <http://www.entrepreneur.com/article/225468>. [27 February 2013].

28 | DEALING WITH ADVANCED PERSISTENT THREATS

WHAT ARE ADVANCED PERSISTENT THREATS?

Attackers look for the weakest link in the organizational security system and follow the path of least resistance. Usually, cybercriminals take advantage of the poor practices of key and certificate management to infect systems with malware that either siphon off information or even plant weaponized code that inflicts physical damage.

Compromised certificates authenticate the malware on the network making it appear as legitimate code. The operating system then allows the malware to install itself without any warning and remain undetected as a persistent threat.

WHAT HAPPENS IN A PERSISTENT ATTACK?

The root of the failure is not the advanced technology that the attackers have used, but the lack of proper controls over the technology that has made the system vulnerable. Cybercriminals are fully aware that each unaccounted and unmanaged certificate and cryptographic key deployed in the organization is a potential exploitable asset.

Such trust-based attacks on an organization can leave deep impacts. Most cybercriminals find it easier to use encryption keys and digital certificates to launch attacks on organizations in order to steal information. Since the defense systems trust the certificates and encryption keys used, they make a perfect vehicle for the organized groups to slide past the defenses. Stolen and weak certificates form the most common tools for authentication of malware planted in the network, as the defenses do not detect them as a threat and that allows the operating system to accept them as legitimate programs.

Most enterprises do not know how many certifications and keys are in use. Venafi at RSA 2013[8] found most organizations managing more than 17,000 encryption keys to be doing it manually. If a digitally signed malware were to attack such an organization, it would take at least a day if not more, to correct the compromise. Moreover, when the attack comes from a trusted code, it defeats the system's ability and capacity to respond quickly to the attack. This makes the trust-base the perfect environment for advanced persistent attacks. The financial impact for such APT exploits can easily be imagined.

HOW TO AVOID SUCH ADVANCED PERSISTENT ATTACKS

The first step in self-defense must be to understand your own position. Without a clear understanding of the inventory of its certificates and keys, the entire organization is exposed to targeted and persistent attacks through trust-based exploits of its intellectual property.

Gaining entry with a stolen encrypted key, an attacker can easily collect unencrypted data from the network. Therefore, the next step would be to encrypt the internal data, similar to the protection provided to data that is sent out.

The enterprise must use a key and certificate management solution to manage the lifecycle securely of all the cryptographic keys used. This must be an automated system that can respond quickly to compromise and limit the amount of financial and reputational damage in case of an attack.

REFERENCES:

1. Rouse, M., Search Security, *advanced persistent threat (APT)*. Available from: <http://searchsecurity.techtarget.com/definition/advanced-persistent-threat-APT>. [Nov 2010].

2. Hudson, J., Help Net Security, *Plugging the trust gap.* Available from: <http://www.net-security.org/article.php?id=1843>. [27 May 2013].

3. Cobb, M., Dark Reading, *Advanced Persistent Threats: The New Reality*. Available from: <http://www.darkreading.com/vulnerability/advanced-persistent-threats-the-new-real/240154502>. [9 May 2013].

29 | OPEN STANDARDS FOR SECURITY IN THE CLOUD

WHAT ARE THE RISKS OF WORKING WITH CLOUDS?

Today, many organizations are under pressure to reduce IT costs by optimizing IT operations. One means of doing this, cloud computing, is a viable means of creating a dynamic, easily deployable resource for operating platforms, development environments, applications, backup and storage capabilities, and many more IT functions. However, a huge number of security considerations present themselves when information security personnel evaluate the risks of cloud computing.

Working with clouds, the primary issue is the loss of control over applications, systems and data security. The cloud does not have many of the existing best practice security controls that the information security professionals rely upon at present. In addition, they are stripped down in many ways, or are uncontrollable by the security teams. For doing business with the Cloud Service Providers or CSPs, the security professionals need to be deeply involved with the development of the language of contract and Service Level Agreements or SLAs.

The next issue pertains to the compounding of compliance and auditing concerns. Audit reporting and compliance verifications within the CSP environments may be infrequent and less in-depth against the requirements of audit and security teams.

The range of cloud computing begins from Software as a Service or SaaS, going up to Infrastructure as a Service or IaaS, with many others in between. Each of these delivery models have an entirely separate set of security conditions to be met, and these are coupled with the different type of cloud services offered, namely public, private and hybrid. Security issues within each of these models have their own risks that need mitigation.

HOW SECURE ARE THE CLOUDS?

Just as there are less or more secure local data centers, there are also less or more secure cloud environments. Studies have shown that most of the fuss is more about insecure web applications rather than about the cloud itself. Web applications suffer security exploits such as cross-site scripting and SQL injections, while cloud-based security tools fared better with fewer malware incidents.

Most enterprises shopping for cloud services would do well to seek clear and compelling answers to key questions such as:

- How is the data stored in the cloud structure encrypted, both when in use and at rest?

- Does the cloud have fine-grained access controls in place?

- How much redundancy does the cloud infrastructure have?

- How well are the web applications protected on the cloud?

ARE OPEN CLOUDS BETTER?

Enterprise cloud computing is at present divided between open and closed or proprietary approaches. Apart from data portability and cloud interoperability amongst the open standards, they have superior benefits for user identity, authentication and security intelligence as compared to proprietary clouds.

Open standards such as Security Assertion Markup Language (SAML) and OAuth allow users to establish identities across multiple platforms. For example, while booking travel arrangements, one login to an employee Intranet is sufficient to identify the user as authorized to book complete transactions for air travel, hotel and car rental with the preset policies,

REFERENCES:

1. Strom, D., tom's Hardware, *How Secure Is The Cloud?* Available from: <http://www.tomshardware.com/reviews/cloud-computing-security,2829.html>. [22 December 2010].

2. The SANS Institute, *SEC524: Cloud Security Fundamentals*. Available from: <http://www.sans.org/course/cloud-security-fundamentals>. [2013].

3. Nagaratnam, N., Help Net Security, *Open standards are key for security in the cloud*. Available from: <http://www.net-security.org/article.php?id=1812>. [5 March 2013].

30 | TARGETED BOTNET ATTACKS AND YOUR RESPONSE

Since 15 April 2013, more than 90,000 computers have together attacked the WordPress website hosted by Cloud-Flare and Hostgator. All users of WordPress, with username "admin" were targeted and more than 10 million random passwords were tried every minute to gain access to their accounts. This targeted attack of the botnets is one of the most powerful ever to be waged on WordPress.

WHAT ARE BOTNETS?

Cyber criminals infiltrate a computer by placing a malware inside it. That turns the computer into a bot, also called a drone or a zombie. The malware resides within the operating system, camouflaging itself from the anti-virus and anti-malware security programs and multiplying itself whenever files from the infected computer are transferred to another computer, infecting the second computer as well. Very soon, it infects several computers in a row and connects all of them via the Internet to form a botnet, which then comes under the control of the botmaster.

HOW BOTNETS AFFECT COMPUTERS

Botnets use a coordinated brute force attack, flooding the targeted server with countless login requests. The botnets try various combinations of usernames and passwords to gain entry, and own the user's accounts they can break into. The attack usually slows down the servers and users on the server are locked out of their websites. This is called the DDoS or the Direct Denial of Service. As WordPress users are given a username "Admin" while they use a password of their own choice, the botnet that attacked the WordPress servers went after users who had not changed their original username.

Once a computer is compromised, it forms another bot and becomes a part of the botnet. The botmaster can extract any information from the compromised machine. Impressive numbers of computers in a targeted attack have the ability to inflict real damage. A single IP or a few IPs can be easily blocked out, but it becomes a different matter when a substantially large number of IPs (above 90,000 in the attack on WordPress) are involved. Attack from multiple computers can be timed to occur several times a second (trying as many as over two billion passwords an hour), overwhelming the security at the server they have targeted.

WHY DO BOTNETS ATTACK COMPUTER SERVERS?

Botnets are constantly trying to increase their numbers so that they can create the condition of an overwhelming flood when they attack. In their quest for adding more computers to their botnets, botmasters target servers with more users attached. Botmasters went after Wordpress as, unlike most home computers, servers hosting WordPress blogs are some of the best in processing power.

Any botmaster setting up a botnet seeks powerful computers. A botnet of such computers can be far more powerful than a regular home-computer constituted botnet, and can then launch DDoS attacks of far greater intensity than what is normally witnessed.

More than 60 million websites around the world are hosted on WordPress, and botmasters would have tremendous computing power if they were able to control even a fraction of these sites.

HOW CAN YOU PREVENT YOUR OWN SITE FROM BEING COMPROMISED BY BOTNETS?

Although the botnets use brute force to try to gain control, it is relatively easy to hold them off. In the case of WordPress users, they had to change their username from "admin" to something different, and at the same time, make their passwords stronger by using a combination of numbers, letters and special characters.

Use of two-step authentication can be another deterrent against botnet attacks. Although it increases the annoyance while logging on to sites like WordPress, it makes it easier for the servers to detect that you are not a bot before they log you on. This makes your site far more secure.

CloudFlare, the server that hosts WordPress, offers free plans that guarantee automatic block for any login attempt that looks like it is from a botnet.

Use the latest released version of the application, as WordPress has already blocked security holes that attackers were exploiting.

REFERENCES:

1. BBC, News Technology, *WordPress website targeted by hackers.* Available from: <http://www.bbc.co.uk/news/technology-22152296>. [15 April 2013].

2. Wheately, M., siliconANGLE, *How To Sidestep The Word-Press Botnet Hack.* Available from: <http://siliconangle.com/blog/2013/04/15/how-to-sidestep-the-word-press-botnet-hack/>. [15 April 2013].

3. Vincent, J., The Independent, *$500 million botnet Citadel attacked by Microsoft and the FBI.* Available from: <http://www.independent.co.uk/life-style/gadgets-and-tech/news/500-million-botnet-citadel-attacked-by-microsoft-and-the-fbi-8647594.html>. [6 June 2013].

31 | SECURITY CHALLENGES OF SCADA

WHAT IS SCADA AND WHAT ARE THE SECURITY CHALLENGES IT FACES?

In the US, as in Europe and the UK, SCADA driven systems connect to the Internet. The Supervisory Control and Data Acquisition or SCADA is the foundation of several industrial automation and control systems. SCADA development started in the 1960s, and preceded the PCs by about two decades. Industrial systems requiring a high degree of computerized control use SCADA-based systems and include chemical plants, energy power plants, and electricity supply grids among many others that demand a hundred percent system availability.

Although many organizations claim they run mission critical IT processes, in reality, SCADA control systems are the real mission critical, as they form the backbone of the national infrastructure.

For example, if the power grid fails, the country as a whole faces a loss of several hundreds of millions of dollars per hour. In addition, this also places countless number of people's lives at stake because of non-operating hospital equipment, air traffic and other civic amenities.

Earlier, SCADA systems connected to the Internet via dial-up modems that had password security, which at that time was highly resistant to attack. Now, they connect via standard Ethernet connection or via Wi-Fi, which is worse. Most of the connections lack proper encryption and authentication, opening them to security challenges.

An analysis of the SCADA security reveals three primary issues:

- Unsecured data or command transmission;
- Open public network connections;
- Technology standardization.

Since SCADA technology evolved earlier, information security was never a part of the design. The data and command transmissions are therefore unsecured and mostly unencrypted. Potential attackers can very easily intercept and issue malicious commands to critical control systems.

Earlier SCADA systems used proprietary communication protocol and closed network systems, which led to a false sense of security. With recent advances, however, interfaces with the Internet are now common, leading to the same malicious threats that other systems on the Internet face regularly.

Newer SCADA systems are adopting more commonly used standard hardware and software, making them vulnerable to the same threats that afflict other systems on the corporate networks.

HOW CAN SCADA SYSTEMS BE MADE MORE SECURE?

Security managers at institutes that use SCADA need to begin to address the challenges by implementing already proven sound information-security practices. Some of the initiatives they must take up are:

- Implement strong encryption over the entire SCADA communications network, including encryption of control commands and monitored data;

- Implement security features on the devices on the network such as authentication and use secure protocols;

- Secure the network by having only the necessary connections to external networks and identify them, including corporate LANs and WANs and other wireless networks;

- Harden the SCADA environment by removing all unnecessary services for the hosts on the network. Also, patch up all systems and keep them up to date;

- Conduct regular security audits and ensure all security practices and procedures are defined and implemented;

- Implement real-time threat protection using intrusion-prevention systems that perform application-layer inspections.

REFERENCES:

1. Yee, A., Computerworld, *How to meet the SCADA security challenge*. Available from: <http://www.computerworld.com/s/article/100204/How_to_meet_the_SCADA_security_challenge>. [8 March 2005].

2. Prince, B., Vulnerability Management, *Google Building Management System Hack Highlights SCADA Security Challenges*. Available from: <http://www.darkreading.com/vulnerability/google-building-management-system-hack-h/240154553>. [9 May 2013].

3. Lieberman, P., Help Net Security, *The SCADA security challenge*. Available from: <http://www.net-security.org/article.php?id=1814>. [7 March 2013].

32 | PROTECTING AGAINST MOBILE DEVICE AND WIRELESS NETWORK ATTACKS

The RSA Conference at San Francisco recently discussed the most significant types of attacks that enterprises are now facing. It emerged that enterprises are facing increasing threats to mobile devices as attackers are taking advantage of the insecure consumer handsets, making them a pivot point for increasing their intrusions into the networks of enterprises.

As an example to one of the threats, one of the discussions was about how attackers pull down apps from one Android Marketplace, introduce a backdoor into it and sell it at another Android app store for a lower price. Even the Apple App Store is not foolproof against these malicious mobile applications, although it is difficult to bypass Apple's vetting process.

HOW IS AN ATTACK ON A MOBILE DEVICE A THREAT TO THE ENTERPRISE?

Attacks on mobile devices themselves, are not a direct threat to the enterprises. However, it becomes so when the attackers use the mobile devices to target the wired networks of enterprises. At this point, the mobile device becomes a real pivot vector. With different makes of mobile devices being available such as Apple, RIM, Android and Microsoft, the security models these organizations use for their products may have to be changed.

Attackers are now using sophisticated methods to infiltrate the network of enterprises. For instance, they package an iPhone with a high capacity battery and send it to their target organization via mail. Even if the package remains unopened, and the organization allows ad-hoc wireless connectivity to mobile devices, the iPhone will simply connect to the network and compromise it. The attacker then has a wide-open access to the network of their target enterprise.

Most attacks on mobile gadgets and wireless networks are successful since enterprises are not very restrictive in providing access to mobile devices. A reason for this is the demand from executives to allow unencumbered BYOD or bring-your-own-devices and allow them access to network resources.

WHAT ARE THE OTHER THREATS TO ENTERPRISES THROUGH THEIR WIRELESS NETWORKS?

Attackers take pride in their accomplishments and show it to the world. They attack the enterprise through hactivism, IPv6 and DNS. Most attackers use basic, easy-to-use tools to explore and exploit the weaknesses of their adversaries' defenses.

HOW TO THWART ATTACKS ON MOBILES AND WIRELESS NETWORKS

For wireless network security, the use of WLAN switches plays a major role. The switches can manage access to hundreds of points and are indispensable when setting up a secure enterprise wireless network.

For securing mobile devices in a better way, the enterprise must adopt a policy for deployment of secure mobile devices. A template for mobile device configuration helps in this regard. Additionally, the enterprise must also create a process for evaluating the mobile apps that could be used within the enterprise. The IT department can make sure the interaction of the device with the app makes functional sense. Administrators can keep their networks safe from the security threats coming from mobile devices, prevent spread of malware, and stop data theft, while the employees continue to use their devices.

In addition, the enterprise must employ a robust and secure wireless infrastructure. For more security, a segmented wireless network may be dedicated exclusively for mobile devices not cleared by the enterprise. The cost of a potential breach may be discussed as a strong point with decision makers within the enterprise to get them to agree on a separate wireless network.

Attackers are now using sophisticated malware to maintain connection with the DNS servers as long as the machine is able to resolve Internet domain names. Therefore, it is im-

portant to look for unusual DNS traffic and frequent bar-
rages of requests on the Internet to unusual destinations.

Use of intrusion detection systems, malware detection systems and firewalls must be included in the network configuration and kept up-to-date for a defense-in-depth approach.

REFERENCES:

1. Eric B. Parizo, E. B., SearchSecurity, *Mobile device attacks to enable more enterprise network intrusions.* Available from: <http://searchsecurity.techtarget.com/news/2240118712/Mobile-device-attacks-to-enable-more-enterprise-network-intrusions>. [29 February 2012].

2. Phifer, L., Search Customization, *Handheld and mobile device security: Mobile malware, breach prevention.* Available from: <http://searchconsumerization.techtarget.com/tutorial/Handheld-and-mobile-device-security-Mobile-malware-breach-prevention>. [Feb 2010].

3. Gonsalves, A. Data Protection, *Mobile devices set to become next DDoS attack tool.* Available from: <http://www.csoonline.com/article/725382/mobile-devices-set-to-become-next-ddos-attack-tool>. [4 January 2013].

33 | MAINTAINING DATA RECOVERY CAPABILITY

WHY IS DATA RECOVERY CAPABILITY NECESSARY?

On compromised machines, attackers often make significant changes to the security configuration and software. Attackers also potentially jeopardize organizational effectiveness by polluting the information content of the organization's databank, making subtle alterations to the data stored there.

When the attack is discovered, it becomes difficult for the organization to remove all traces of the attacker's presence on the network if the organization has no credible data recovery capability.

WHAT HAPPENS IF DATA RECOVERY CAPABILITY IS ABSENT?

Among the many assets belonging to an organization, data is the most important. For any daily activity, it is impossible for an organization to continue meaningful and efficient operations without using its database. Without recourse to recovery of unpolluted or lost data, any organization is as good as "gone".

Today, when most businesses are technology-dependent, even minor disruptions can render IT systems and highly sophisticated machinery ineffective. For example, a production floor employing tens of networked pick-n-place SMD robots can chalk up losses amounting to several thousands of dollars within minutes simply because of a corrupt database.

In the absence of a reliable backup and data recovery, the entire plant is rendered non-productive, further adding to the losses. In fact, a consulting and research firm reports that almost two out of five enterprises that face such physical disasters run out of steam and shut shop within five years, regardless of their size.

HOW TO INITIATE AND MAINTAIN DATA RECOVERY CAPABILITY

To implement a data recovery strategy, an organization must evaluate two key parameters. One is the RTO, which is the downtime or the time the organization can bear to be without a particular IT system or a resource. The other is the RPO or the amount of loss the organization can withstand after restoration from backups.

For shorter Recovery Objectives, the solution is expensive: the organization develops a faster responding plan to perform more frequent data backups. On the other hand, longer Recovery Objectives, although cheaper, will result in slower responses and will require fewer data backups. The goal is to resume operation with the minimum of disruption.

Apart from affecting the organization's capability to recover data quickly and effectively, appropriate determination of RPO and RTO will optimize the organization's investments in data-backup solutions.

Many solutions exist at different levels and different forms to implement data backup. Depending on the sensitivity of the data in use, hardware solutions such as tapes and tape drives, raid solutions, and multiple hard drives in conjunction with suitable software must be used.

For extremely sensitive data, the organization may have to invest in a multiple off-site back-up solution. For greater protection, the data being stored should also be encrypted as it is being backed up.

Data recovery strategy of the organization must also involve testing the backups periodically to verify usefulness in case of an actual attack.

REFERENCES:

1. The SANS Institute, *Critical Control 8: Data Recovery Capability*. Available from: <http://www.sans.org/critical-security-controls/control.php?id=8>. [2013].

2. Baccam, T., SANS IT Audit, *Critical Control 19: Data Recovery Capability*. Available from: <http://it-audit.sans.org/blog/2010/05/19/critical-control-19-data-recovery-capability>. [19 May 2010].

3. XDataBackup, *Importance of Data Recovery*. Available from: <http://www.xbackup.net/data-recovery-importance.html>. [2006].

34 | STRATEGIC MALWARE DEFENSE

WHAT IS MALWARE?

Malware is malicious software that has now become a dangerous aspect and an integral part of threats from the Internet. Organizations and end-users become targets via browsing of the net, attachments to emails, using the cloud and other vectors including the mobile devices.

HOW MALWARE WORKS

Malicious software and code can tamper with and change the contents of a system. It can capture sensitive data while infecting other systems on the network. Modern malware has evolved beyond the behavioral and signature-based detection of most anti-virus tools and may have the capability to disable the tools monitoring the system. System administrators use Anti-malware tools, comprising anti-spyware and anti-virus tools to defend against the threats from malware.

EXTENT OF DAMAGE CAUSED BY MALWARE

Depending on the targets of the virus, the damage to an infected computer on a network can vary: from sending out spam, to a complete breakdown of the network or critical data loss.

Cost is one way of measuring the detrimental effects of malware. The cost to the global economy is as much as $1 trillion a year from cybercriminals using malware to steal personal data such as credit card information. That means the individual business must spend an average of $3.8 million in reacting to, containing, and cleaning up after a malware attack. Per incident, the average loss for a customer affected by malware works out to be about $1,000, and this figure excludes the fear and loss of trust that accompanies a cyber-crime.

Malware lodged in your website can blacklist your site by search engines such as Google. It may take up to 13 days on average to be removed from the blacklist. During this time, customers see warnings that your site is unsafe, forcing them to move toward your competitor's business. That means nearly two weeks of lost sales because of decreased traffic. .

Apart from the involvement of cost and loss in sales, malware attacks can be more damaging as the reputation of your business may be hit seriously. Even one lost potential customer (seeing the blacklist warning) may spread the word that your site (read business) cannot be trusted. With tools such as Twitter and Facebook, it takes only seconds for this mistrust to spread to thousands of people. Therefore, even if you were at best only a victim of malware attack, you risk losing sales and reputation.

BEST PRACTICES TO THWART MALWARE ATTACKS

Aside from taking a holistic approach for the overall security of the network, different classes of threats require different defenses. Specifically for malware, protection of the web-server is the predominant approach.

The latest trend is toward adding a protection layer that works at the website level. Anti-malware scanning from a cloud-based service is emerging as the most powerful and effective supplement to web server security implemented in the traditional manner.

The service conducts regular scans to detect hidden malware in web pages facing the customer and alerts the website owners if any malware is found. Features include changing scanning speed and frequency, using databases to keep track of threats, varying reporting capabilities, dynamic updates and integration with related tools.

REFERENCES:

1. The SANS Institute, *Twenty Critical Security Controls for Effective Cyber Defense.* Available from: <http://www.sans.org/critical-security-controls/>. [2013].

2. Kaspersky, *Damage caused by malware.* Available from: <http://www.securelist.com/en/threats/detect?chapter=76>. [1997].

3. Symantec, WHITE PAPER: *How Malware Infects Websites and Harms Businesses —and What You Can Do to Stop It.* Available from: <http://www.geotrust.com/anti-malware-scan/malware-threat-white-paper.pdf>. [2012].

35 | SECURE CONFIGURATIONS VIGILANCE

THE EXTENT OF THE THREAT

When attackers have compromised both the external and internal networks of an enterprise, they usually install automated computer attack programs that constantly scan the target networks. These programs search for systems that have vulnerable software installed in the default configuration, as delivered from resellers and manufacturers.

As default configurations are mostly meant for ease-of-deployment and ease-of-use rather than security, these are exploitable in their default state. Moreover, security patches are not always applied in a planned manner. Software updates too, often introduce unknown weaknesses into vulnerable software that attackers can exploit.

EFFECT ON THE ENTERPRISE

Once attackers have gained access to the network, they are able to trespass within, approach, store data in the system or retrieve data from it, communicate with, intercept, interfere or change the system at will.

It is easy for them to obstruct the network services by planting malicious programs and overload the resources. This might fill up hard drive storage space, send messages for resetting a host's subnet mask, as well as prevent network resources from accepting network connections.

Attackers can also use the system as a pivot point for invading further into the enterprise. Common forms of attack include distributed denial of service, relay of worms, viruses, or spam and destruction or modification of files.

It is easy for the attackers to plant a program, which is undetectable (such a program is called a Trojan Horse), into an unauthorized application and use it to siphon money from the enterprise accounts or transfer credit card numbers or trade secrets to remote servers.

The risks faced by the enterprise include:

- Unauthorized disclosure of information
- Disruption of computer services
- Loss of productivity
- Financial loss
- Legal implications
- Blackmail

Not only does the enterprise lose confidential and sensitive information, it is also subject to loss of credibility, reputation, competitive edge and market share. Customers, investors or even the public may sue the enterprise for the security or privacy breaches.

HOW CAN THIS THREAT BE MITIGATED?

The best way to avoid security breaches is to prevent them from happening in the first place, by adopting and employing a strong security policy for the enterprise.

Although 100% of breaches or leaks cannot be prevented, it is possible to minimize the damages and remediate effectively. Using secure configuration for all your hardware and software assets along with inventory control and management can help to achieve this.

This also requires proper deployment, maintenance and documentation of layered security architecture for protecting the enterprise network. A layered architecture would include, apart from access controls, firewalls, antivirus tools and encrypted data transmissions, and the advanced analysis and detection capabilities of technology such as sandbox.

By employing sandbox technologies, the enterprise has the knowledge base to detect, identify and to defend against new threats as they arrive and

remediate as necessary. An additional advantage with sandboxing is documenting the steps taken by the enterprise for complying with the guidelines of the SEC breach disclosure.

REFERENCES:

1. Sans Institute, *Critical Control 3: Secure Configurations for Hardware and Software on Mobile Devices, Laptops, Workstations, and Servers.* Available from: <http://www.sans.org/critical-security-controls/control.php?id=3>. [2013].

2. Hau, D., Sans Institute, *Unauthorized Access – Threats, Risk, and Control.* Available from: <http://www.giac.org/paper/gsec/3161/unauthorized-access-threats-risk-control/105264>. [11 July 2013].

3. Threattracksecurity.com, *Enterprise security white paper sandboxing helps avoid security breach.* Available from: <http://www.threattracksecurity.com/documents/enterprise-security-white-paper-sandboxing-helps-avoid-security-breach.pdf>. [2013].

36 | 2-FACTOR AUTHENTICATION

WHAT IS 2-FACTOR AUTHENTICATION?

Most of us are used to the username/password combination that we enter into websites for paying our bills, reading our mails, shopping, or storing our music and or photos. However, with the growing sophistication of applications on the net and the proliferation of cyber crooks, the present state of online authentication is unable to meet the security needs of consumers and businesses.

Large-scale web services are therefore, adding another layer of complexity to the login experience. This is the 2-factor authentication, where, in addition to the username/password combination, you have to furnish information, which becomes the second factor.

HOW DOES 2-FACTOR AUTHENTICATION WORK?

Criminals are easily able to steal username/password combinations to gain access to a user's data for committing frauds, mostly of a financial nature. In the case of an enterprise, the attack also includes stealing commercial information such as intellectual property.

Two-factor authentication, also known as TFA or 2FA, adds a second step of verification or an extra layer of security. This is also a "multi-factor authentication", as this extra step requires something that is only available from the user alone; for example, a biometric fingerprint, a physical token, or the answer to a secret question. (what was your mother's maiden name?) Of course, the answer or the authentication to be provided must have been supplied to the website earlier when first setting up the account. The website crosschecks your entry with the information available in its database and lets you in only if there is a match.

WHAT IS THE ADVANTAGE OF 2-FACTOR AUTHENTICATION?

The fact that you are using another piece of information that is known only to you or can be furnished only by you, makes it that much harder for a potential attacker to gain access to your account and steal your identity or your personal finances.

With a 2-factor authentication, cybercriminals now need more information than simply the username/password combination. This helps to lower the number of cases where accounts have been broken into, and the instances of phishing via emails.

Some banks and other institutions have used hardware tokens for 2-factor authentication. The downside of this arrangement is tokens have to be issued and the user must wait to gain access to their private data. Moreover, being small, the tokens are sometimes lost, causing more headaches when customers request replacements.

As an alternative, mobile phone SMS technology is currently being used for 2-factor authentication, and this is working very well. Turning a mobile phone into an instrument for authentication is a logical step, as there are more than 5 billion of them in use. Once you enter your primary authentication and it verifies, you receive an SMS on your mobile containing a one-time and time-limited number. Your authentication is completed when you enter the number and it matches with the number that was sent to you.

The authentication number sent to you is valid only for one entry, and remains alive only for a limited amount of time, for example, for 10-20 minutes. This makes it more difficult for the clandestine attacker trying to get into your account.

REFERENCES:

1. SecurEnvoy, *What is 2FA?* Available from: <http://www.securenvoy.com/two-factor-authentication/what-is-2fa.shtm>. [2012].

2. Dunkelberger, P., HelpNet Security, *The future of online authentication*. Available from: <http://www.net-security.org/article.php?id=1849>. [10 June 2013].

3. Rosenblatt, S., Cnet, *Two-factor authentication: What you need to know (FAQ)*. Available from: <http://news.cnet.com/8301-1009_3-57586014-83/two-factor-authentication-what-you-need-to-know-faq/>. [23 May 2013].

37

INS AND OUTS OF CAPTCHA RE-RIDING ATTACKS

WHAT IS A CAPTCHA RE-RIDING ATTACK?

Many web sites want to distinguish whether it is a robot that is reading the site or a human, mostly to avoid the spread of spam. They use a system called CAPTCHA, which is an acronym for Completely Automated Public Turing Test to tell Computers and Humans Apart. The website has distorted text on the page, which can only be read by humans.

There are two types of CAPTCHA, one with a single word and one with two words. They mostly use old type fonts with deliberately introduced distortions to make it almost impossible for any OCR (Optical Character Recognition) to recognize. Therefore any automated system will not be able to bypass the CAPTCHA test. Websites use CAPTCHA when they want to avoid bogus memberships or hoax accounts. Some of the money related websites use it when creating new accounts. Some websites may test you with a

CAPTCHA if you have entered a wrong password two or three times.

Attackers use the CAPTCHA re-riding attack to bypass the CAPTCHA protection, which the web applications adapt. In an HTTP session, the code for verifying the CAPTCHA solution sent by the user does not clear it; the attackers may exploit the situation. They use the same CAPTCHA solution to repeatedly send requests to the website.

WHAT HAPPENS DURING A CAPTCHA RE-RIDING ATTACK?

When a user visits a webpage and requests a registration the website creates an HTTP session, assigns it a session ID, and presents the registration page to the user along with the session ID inside a cookie. The registration page also has a tag, which directs the visitor's browser to a remote server to retrieve a CAPTCHA to be displayed on the screen.

The visitor's browser follows the instructions in the tag and sends a request to the remote server for the CAPTCHA. Accordingly, the server creates a new CAPTCHA with a random text and its solution, stores it for the current HTTP session and sends out the CAPTCHA image to the requesting client browser, to be displayed there.

The user solves the CAPTCHA and the browser sends the solution to the server for verification. The server retrieves its own solution from the HTTP session and verifies the solution with that provided by the client.

If the two solutions match, the client is given the clearance to proceed to the next logical step in the registration process; if the visitor's response doesn't match the CAPTCHA image, the registration process starts afresh.

During the verification process, the CAPTCHA solution remains inside the HTTP session and it is not cleared for as long as the session is alive. This is true if the verification succeeds and the user is cleared to the next step. If the verification fails, the web applications continue to use the same session ID and the same HTTP session. The attacker exploits this situation.

The attacker can solve the CAPTCHA and send the solution to the website, recording the submission using a web proxy. Using a custom script, or a tool such as Burp Intruder, he can send this request multiple times. With each request, he changes the User ID and is able to create multiple new accounts using the same single CAPTCHA solution, thus defeating the very purpose of having the CAPTCHA in the first place.

Instead of directly using them, attackers are exploiting the vulnerabilities to provide tools and data to others for illegal activities. Using such attacks, millions of harvested emails are often put up for sale, and these contain data related to military, government and intelligence agencies.

HOW TO PREVENT A CAPTCHA RE-RIDING ATTACK

Two major steps can prevent CAPTCHA re-riding attacks:

- Never trust emails from unknown recipients offering something you did not request and demanding your information;

- Reset the CAPTCHA solution within the HTTP session as soon as the CAPTCHA verification stage completes.

REFERENCES:

1. Kalra, G. S., Open Security Research, *CAPTCHA Re-Riding Attack*. Available from: <http://blog.opensecurityresearch.com/2012/02/captcha-re-riding-attack.html>. [28 February 2012].

2. Paganini, P., Security Affairs, *The offer of Russian underground for phishing campaigns*. Available from: <http://securityaffairs.co/wordpress/12756/cyber-crime/the-offer-of-russian-underground-for-phishing-campaigns.html>. [9 March 2013].

3. Kalra, G. S., Blackhat.com, *Bypassing CAPTCHAs by Impersonating CAPTCHA Providers*. Available from: <https://media.blackhat.com/bh-us-12/Arsenal/Kalra/BH_US_12_Kalra_Bypassing_CAPTCHAs_by_Impersonating_CAPTCHA_Providers_WP.pdf>. [28 February 2012].

38 | DOS ATTACK SECURITY STRATEGIES

WHAT IS A DOS ATTACK?

Rogue attackers usually target web servers with intent to disrupt services. Users are prevented from connecting to the server for an online application or service, and this is commonly termed as denial of service or DOS. When multiple hosts are compromised in this manner, it is called DDOS or distributed denial of service.

Typical targets for a DOS attack are firewalls, routers, application servers, DNS servers and Web servers. Attackers create the DOS conditions by impairing the server itself or by consuming the bandwidth of the server.

As more companies conduct their businesses online, DOS/ DDOS attacks are increasing, leading to severe losses in finance and productivity. The enormity of the problem can be judged by the Verisign survey of IT decision makers, which revealed that more than 60% of the respondents had sustained an attack of DOS in the past year, and more than 10% of these had been hit six or more times. More than 50% of those attacked reported downtime, which resulted in revenue loss.

REPERCUSSIONS OF A DOS ATTACK

The denial of service attack usually spans several entry points or vectors on the network simultaneously. Most often, attackers rope in multiple compromised PCs, which then act as zombies. Botnets or armies of zombie PCs then inject malware such as viruses, Trojans and spam into the network.

This activity multiplies into generating multiple gigabytes-per-second of network traffic, creating large scale distributed denial of service, clogging the access network and denying service to legitimate users. As a consequence, business operations and revenue are severely undermined.

Apart from revenue loss and downtime, DOS attacks lead to devastating effects for many businesses. This usually takes the form of a downward plunge in brand reputation, bottom line and customer relationships. Times are changing, and attackers are resorting to advanced forms of DOS attacks. Most traditional approaches to counter such attacks with intrusion prevention system devices, firewalls and over-provisioning of bandwidth no longer work, leaving the services, applications and networks of an organization unprotected.

SOME USEFUL METHODS TO KEEP YOUR NETWORK SAFE FROM DOS ATTACKS

- Incorporate normal redundancy, use more servers spread around many datacenters, and use good load balancing;

- Lock down your DNS servers, use enhanced DNS protection, and similar load balancing as already in use for your web and other resources;

- Set up good firewalls, let routers drop junk packets and block ICMP;

- Plan to replace dynamic resources quickly with static ones.

Having more servers helps to spread the load, provided you have large pipes to handle all the traffic; as large as your financial resources will allow.

Even if your website is not being attacked, an attack on the DNS servers is as bad. If one is able to resolve your DNS name and connect to your DNS servers, they will be able to reach your website. That means your DNS servers must be protected with the same thoroughness as your other resources.

When you are managing your own network and serving your own data, you must take the protection to the network layer. For example, your website is never going to generate random queries to your DNS servers. Therefore, you may safely block all UDP port 53 packets from reaching your servers.

Despite the precautions, some attacks may filter through, and you must be prepared to mitigate the threat. Often the target of the attack is the database or some custom scripts you are running. Use of caching servers and providing static content can help if you are under attack.

REFERENCES:

1. Verisign, *What Is a DDoS Attack?* Available from: <http://www.verisigninc.com/en_US/products-and-services/network-intelligence-availability/ddos/ddos-attack/index.xhtml>. [2011].

2. AT&T, *Denial of Service - DDoS Protection.* Available from: <http://www.business.att.com/enterprise/Service/network-security/threat-vulnerability-management/ddos-protection/>. [29 June 2013].

3. Lambert, P., TechRepublic, *DDoS attack methods and how to prevent or mitigate them.* Available from: <http://www.techrepublic.com/blog/security/ddos-attack-methods-and-how-to-prevent-or-mitigate-them/8523>. [15 October 2012].

39 | CROSS SITE PORT SCANNING BASICS

WHAT IS CROSS SITE PORT SCANNING?

Several websites provide functionality to access data from other web applications facing the Internet, to verify application availability or for internal use. For example, applications can:

- access images with user specified URLs,

- show server status against user specified URLs,

- manifest files, XML

- pull feeds.

With a Cross Side Port Scan or XSPS, an attacker can abuse the above functionality of the web application and send specially modified queries to a remote web server. This issue has been identified in prominent web applications on the Internet, including Adobe, Yahoo, Pinterest, Facebook, Mozilla, StatMyWeb, Apigee, Google and several others.

The attacker analyzes the response received. For unique responses, he may try a blind port scan on the Internet facing device on the same server or host or event on internal local networks.

WHAT HAPPENS DURING A CROSS SIDE PORT SCAN ATTACK?

When an application sitting between the server and the client does not verify or sanitize the backend response sent by the remote server before displaying it to the client, the application is vulnerable to attacks from cross side port scanning.

An attacker can craft special messages and send them through the web application to the remote server to study its responses. Based on the responses received, the attacker can grab banners, fingerprint internal network aware services, exploit vulnerable programs, identify web application frameworks and vulnerabilities, listen on internal networks, run code on reachable machines, read local files and much more.

Most social networking sites allow a user to input a link pointing to an external image, which is present on a third party server. For example, users can update their profile image by either specifying a URL to the image hosted somewhere on the Internet or by uploading the image from their computer. In a utopian world, the user is expected to enter a valid URL pointing to the image.

The social networking site downloads the image on its server, recreates the URL and presents the image to its users. If the original user has removed the image and it is no longer available at the user supplied URL, the social networking site informs its other users. The social networking web application generates error messages to inform the users that the URL has been removed.

The error messages sent contain a huge amount of information about the server side. An attacker can analyze the unique error messages, response byte size, and response times to identify port status. He can then initiate port scanning of the remote server using the vulnerable web application.

HOW TO FIX CROSS SIDE PORT SCANNING ATTACKS

XSPA attacks may be thwarted in multiple ways to mitigate the vulnerability:

- Response handling – Validate the responses received from the remote server. Before processing or displaying the data to the client, make sure the data received satisfies all the checks imposed on the server by the application.

- Error handling and messages – When displaying the messages to the client use only generic error messages. Use generic messaging even if the server sends invalid data to a request.

- Restrict the connectivity to HTTP ports – Strip the input URL of any port specifications and use only the port determined by the protocol handler.

- Blacklist all internal IP addresses so web applications will not be able to use them to fetch data. This will protect the server from a one-time attack vector.

- Disable all unwanted protocols and use only http and https to make requests to remote servers; whitelist only these so that web applications will not make requests over other protocols.

REFERENCES:

1. Walikar, R., sched.org, *Cross Site Port Scanning*. Available from: <http://appsecusa2012.sched.org/event/8969ba d647d2f92442df3f66617018c5#.Ucp1exUt11w>. [25 October 2012].

2. Walikar, R., Mediablackhat.com., *Poking Servers with Facebook*. Available from: <https://media.blackhat. com/ad-12/Walikar/bh-ad-12-pokingserverswith-Facebook-Walikar-WP.pdf>. [15 November 2012].

3. Energy.gov, *V-078: WordPress Bugs Permit Cross-Site Scripting and Port Scanning Attacks.* Available from: <http://energy.gov/cio/articles/v-078-wordpress-bugs-permit-cross-site-scripting-and-port-scanning-attacks>. [28 January 2013].

40 | IDENTIFYING AND PROTECTING AGAINST MOBILE WEB HACKING

WHAT IS MOBILE WEB HACKING?

You may suddenly discover that personal information from your mobile is splattered all over the Internet. Possibly your text messages, your pictures and intimate conversations are available for all to see. Not only is this an invasion of privacy, it may also be extremely damaging to your livelihood and personal life.

In the technologically advanced world, sometimes people want to hack into personal details of others for various reasons. For example, there may be people who you have fallen out with in business or love, people who may dislike you for something you have said or done, or friends who have now become unfriendly. It is prudent to guard your personal information properly, as it is not always possible to predict how some relationships might turn out.

Apart from sour relationships, business rivalry is another reason for mobile web hacking. Your business competitor may want access to your personal information to know what you may be planning next. There may also be the friendly neighborhood attacker who wants to blackmail you over some sensitive information you have in your cellphone. The attacker may also be looking for your financial information to steal from your bank account.

HOW TO DETERMINE IF YOUR MOBILE HAS BEEN HACKED

Most users of mobile devices do not think of their cellphones as computers and hence do not take adequate steps to protect them as they do their PCs and laptops.

Mobile devices are increasingly becoming as powerful and sophisticated as regular computers, and hence are equally vulnerable unless protected adequately. When an attacker compromises a system, he has to tamper with the mobile's system files in some way to prevent detection and to maintain continued access. This may include deleting some files, replacing or altering them, or even adding extra files.

Intrusion detection systems or IDS can warn you if there are attempts by attackers to penetrate your cellphone. Periodic file integrity checking is one method of identifying if your mobile has been hacked and/or compromised by an attacker slipping past your IDS.

People are increasingly using smart mobile phones to visit websites and conduct several types of transactions on the web. It is very easy for attackers to compromise a mobile phone after the user has visited an infected or hacked website.

Detecting an infected site is easy with the Google Webmaster Tool or GWT, which has warnings for malware. When the tool detects malware, it sends warning emails to the webmaster and owners can see the warning when they login via the Webmaster Tool.

HOW CAN YOU PROTECT YOURSELF FROM MOBILE WEB HACKING?

- Download apps only from your phone's store;
- Update to the latest operating system of your phone and the installed apps;
- Always have your firewall turned on;
- Install the latest antivirus software and update it regularly;
- Install the latest antispyware program and update it regularly;
- Never download from suspicious websites;
- Never open suspicious looking attachments to emails;
- Turn on Bluetooth only when necessary;
- Turn off your phone when not in use for long.

It is imperative to treat your phone as a computer and protect it in the same manner. One of the most important tips is to keep your mobile with you always or in a place where you know it will be safe, and not leave it around in a public place. It is also prudent not to store too much sensitive information in your phone, and keep track of what kind of data or photos you maintain.

REFERENCES:

1. Cobb, M., ComputerWeekly.com, *How to detect hacking with a Microsoft file integrity checker*. Available from: <http://www.computerweekly.com/tip/How-to-detect-hacking-with-a-Microsoft-file-integrity-checker>. [Nov 2010].

2. Rana, G., Gogi.in, *How to Detect if your Website is Hacked or Infected*. Available from: <http://www.gogi.in/detect-website-hacked-infected.html>. [7 December 2011].

3. Mardigian-Kiles, T., Webroot, *How to Prevent Phone Hacking and Sleep Like a Baby Again.* Available from: <http://www.webroot.com/En_US/consumer/articles/mobile-how-to-prevent-phone-hacking-and-sleep-like-a-baby-again>. [2004].

41

USING OPEN SOURCE HACKING TOOLS FOR SECURITY AUDITING

Contrary to popular belief, a hacker is not the bad guy who breaks into your computer security to steal your information. Rather, let us think of him as the one who helps to strengthen your computer and your network system security.

Although expensive, there are some great tools on the market which provide an in-depth analysis when snooping around to detect intrusion. The budget–conscious consumer or small enterprise can access a large number of fantastic tools available free of cost, and these are actively developed by the community.

HERE ARE SOME MUST-HAVE HACKING TOOLS:

NETWORK MAPPER (NMAP):

This is a free open source utility you can use to explore your network for security auditing. You can use it for a single host or for rapidly scanning large networks. Network and system administrators use it for conducting network inventory, monitoring host or service uptime and for managing service upgrade schedules.

REMOTE SECURITY SCANNER – NESSUS:

Nessus is an extremely popular vulnerability scanner, which has led to significant savings for many of the world's largest organizations. Most enterprises use it to audit their devices used for business-critical applications. Nessus works within a client-server framework.

WIRESHARK:

If you want to interactively browse and capture the contents of network frames, you can use Wireshark, the open source free network protocol analyzer. This commercial-quality sniffer or analyzer is designed for UNIX and has some special features that are not available even with closed-source (not free) sniffers.

CAIN AND ABEL:

This program helps to exploit vulnerabilities and bugs that can be fixed with little effort. Fundamentally, this is a tool to recover passwords from Microsoft Operating Systems. Any kind of password may be recovered by sniffing the network, including encrypted passwords using Dictionary, Crypt-analysis and Brute-Force methods.

KISMET:

If you are looking for a simple and free wireless network detector, sniffer and an intrusion detector system, you can give Kismet a try. Kismet works on 802.11 layer2 wireless networks. The only requirement is your card must support raw monitoring or rfmon mode.

NETSTUMBLER:

You can detect WLANs or Wireless Local Area Networks using Netstumbler. This is a wireless tool for the Windows operating systems, and its Linux counterpart is much more powerful. Netstumbler helps you set up and verify your network the way you want. It easily detects illegal vulnerable access points in your workplace and locates the areas with poor coverage.

SUPERSCAN:

Superscan is a powerful TCP port scanner, pinger and re-solver. The updated version for Windows is Superscan 4. It also works as an alternative for Nmap on Windows. Another alternative is to use Angry IP Scanner.

NETSLEUTH:

If you want to monitor your network silently to identify and fingerprint network devices, try the open source tool Netsleuth. This is a network forensics and analysis tool, de-signed for situations requiring triage of incident response. Netsleuth monitors your network, provides cyber security and analyzes network forensics. With this tool, it is easy to get a real-time overview of the type of devices and people who are connected to the Ethernet or Wi-Fi network.

Netsleuth can identify a large variety of devices, includ-ing tablets, printers, desktops, tablets and smartphones. It works well with other tools such as Kismet or tcpdump and aids in network forensics and intrusion response.

NIKTO2:

Nikto2 is a scanner for web servers that performs comprehensive tests for multiple items. It can check for version-specific problems in more than 270 types of servers and can detect more than 1200 versions of updated servers. . Nikto2 also detects the presence of multiple index files and HTTP server options.

ETTERCAP:

Ettercap can comprehensively sniff out man-in-the-middle attacks on live connections. It has plenty of features for host and network analysis and supports passive or active dissection of several protocols.

REFERENCES:

1. Security & Hakcing Blog, *Top 15 Free Hacking Tools.* Available from: <http://securityblog.gr/1127/top-15-open-sourcefree-securityhacking-tools/>. [16 Aug 2012].

2. Dangwal, R., Hacky Shacky, *7 Must Have Tools For Every Hacker*. Available from: <http://www.hackyshacky.com/2013/02/Must-have-hacking-tools.html>. [2013].

3. Tools Yard. Available from: <http://toolsyard.thehackernews.com/2012/11/netsleuth-open-source-network-forensics.html#>. [2012].

42 | YOU NEED PATCH MANAGEMENT

WHAT IS PATCH MANAGEMENT?

O ne major time-consumer in business is to keep the infrastructure functional. For most businesses, the IT department spends more than 70% of its time in maintenance and administration, according to recent research from the International Data Corporation (IDC). For some, this figure is even higher, reaching 80% or more.

Updating, maintaining and patching software and systems for the latest security vulnerabilities are now major overhead expenses for IT managers. This is because IT systems are now more complex and distributed, and there is a significant increase in the overhead costs involved in keeping the systems functioning smoothly.

Software manufacturers release patch updates frequently, depending on how fast they are able to overcome vulnerabilities found in their programs. Not only software, but now firmware, development systems and hardware manufacturers also produce updates, and there are patches from software vendors and out-of-band patches to be handled.

WHY SHOULD PATCH MANAGEMENT BE A PRIORITY?

Most business' networks could carry a flaw in their unpatched systems, representing a real security threat. According to the US technology standards body, the NIST, in more than 90% of successful attacks against companies, the attackers exploited vulnerabilities that were already known. All the attacks could have been prevented had the systems been patched correctly and in time.

HOW SHOULD PATCH MANAGEMENT BE HANDLED?

IT departments in a business may decide to let users handle their own patch updates to reduce the company's IT burden. The real situation is not all patches released by their manufacturers install without creating further problems. There is risk of a breakup of critical business processes when users patch their systems with an untested patch. While off-the-shelf software is capable of being thus disrupted, it is more common with highly customized in-house software.

Centralized methods for patch management are therefore quickly catching up with businesses. For large businesses, the sheer numbers of servers, desktop systems, smartphones, tablets and all associated applications make it almost impossible to patch all devices manually. Automated systems of patch management handle such situations with more reliability and increased security.

Automated patch management can take care of the growing number of threats built specifically to attack systems before they are upgraded or patched. Many businesses and their IT security focus on mitigating the zero-day exploits, but human error in manual patching leaves too many systems vulnerable, even long after the patches have been released.

Manual and uncoordinated patching can leave the enterprise in a state of disruption and cause loss through downtime. This is mostly true in the case of patches untested for their compatibility with the operating software.

WHY AUTOMATED PATCHING IS AN ADVANTAGE TO BUSINESSES

Enterprises must implement in-house testing or look at using a patch supplier who also handles testing before applying patches on running systems. Although it does increase patch management cost deployment, the benefits far outweigh the investments due to the reduction in downtime and the consequent lost revenue.

Using automated patch management, the enterprise remains productive and conserves valuable IT resources. Most automated patch management systems can be programmed to implement patching beyond the core working time.

REFERENCES:

1. Lutz, S. Help Net Security, *Automate your way out of patching hell*. Available from: <http://www.net-security.org/article.php?id=1845>.[30 May 2013].

2. Florian, C., TechTalkToMe, *5 Benefits of Automating Patch Management*. Available from: <http://www.gfi.com/blog/5-benefits-automating-patch-management/>. [25 November 2010].

3. Symantec, *Automatic Patch Management*. Available from: <http://www.symantec.com/articles/article.jsp?aid=automating_patch_management>. [8 February, 2005].

43 | PCI 2.0 AND WEB SECURITY

WHAT IS PCI 2.0?

All service providers must be compliant with the Payment Card Industry Data Security Standard, or PCI DSS 2.0. There is no option for ignoring the PCI compliance. Visa can charge non-compliant merchants of level 1 or level 2, who deal with more than 1 million transactions per year, monthly fines ranging from US$5,000 to US$25,000. MasterCard merchants of level 1 and level 2 have to produce a QSA (Qualified Security Assessor) report on compliance starting from 2012.

The objective of PCI is to provide guidelines on the proper methods of storing, processing and transmitting credit card data in electronic format.

STEPS REQUIRED FOR COMPLIANCE WITH PCI 2.0

Service providers and merchants who handle credit card data must download a copy of the self-assessment questionnaire of the PCI. This allows them to assess what security measures are expected from them. They can also request a free scan from one of the Approved Scanning Vendors or ASVs. This will reveal all the gaps in relation to the security level required by PCI. Not all may have the technical skills within the organization to address the gaps, or the list of vulnerabilities may be too long to handle. In such cases, Qualified Security Assessors are available, and hiring them will help in addressing the vulnerabilities.

THE COST OF COMPLIANCE TO PCI 2.0

PCI DSS compliance does not come cheap. However, the final cost depends on several factors such as:

- Your business type;

- Number of transactions you process annually;

- Your existing IT infrastructure;

- Your current practices for storing and processing credit/debit card information.

The Ponemon Institute has found that merchants who undergo audits for ensuring compliance with the PCI DSS standards are paying on average US$225,000 every year.

SO WHAT IS NEW IN PCI 2.0?

There are changes in version 2.0 and every application security tester will need to be aware of them. You will need to identify those applications, which must be compliant to Application Security, the requirement number 6 of PCI. These will be the applications with custom code to handle data from credit cards from both external and internal websites. Other applications that need to be compliant would be those requiring upgrades, updates, patches and maintenance.

As an example, for an application to be compliant with PCI requirement 6.2, you must first conduct a risk-based assessment of vulnerability and then apply any recommended patch or upgrade. Section 6.5 of the standard also requires that you take measures to remove specific vulnerabilities. These include misconfiguration, injection flaws and URL access rights.

According to section 6.6 of PCI requirements, a review of all custom application code is necessary for common vulnerabilities. This review has to be done by an organization specializing in application security. Alternatively, the organization should install a firewall in front of web-facing applications. The alternative arrangement meets the requirement, although it is not a robust control and is only recommended for low-budget situations.

WHAT AREAS IS THE PCI 2.0 LIKELY TO AFFECT?

All cardholder data and its location and flow must be identified and documented through a discovery process to make sure everything is kept in check and identified as important.

Virtualization has now been brought under the ambit of protection. This is important given that anything with a URL or an IP address is vulnerable.

PA-DSS and PCI DSS requirements are now aligned with centralized logging supported by payment applications. Delving deeper into these areas benefits everyone during web security assessments.

References to CERT and SANS CWE Top 25 standards are provided along with additional guidance for 'secure coding'. This is a broader set of industry standards, which will benefit internal auditors, IT managers and QA professionals.

The security assessment process now has a risk-based approach and this includes preventing the common coding mistakes usually introduced during SDLC, which often gave rise to high-risk vulnerabilities.

REFERENCES:

1. Abouchar, D. PCI Compliance Gude, *How to Select a PCI Compliant Service Provider: Advice for Small Business Owners.* Available from: <http://www.pcicomplianceguide.org/merchants-select-pci-compliant-service-provider.php>. [?].

2. Beaver, K., Acunetix, *Notable changes in PCI DSS 2.0 affecting Web application security.* Available from: <http://www.acunetix.com/blog/news/changes-pci-dss-2/>. [18 November 2010].

3. Cerullo F., ComputerWeekly.com, *PCI DSS v2.0: How does it affect your web application security testing?* Available from: <http://www.computerweekly.com/opinion/PCI-DSS-v20-How-does-it-affect-your-web-application-security-testing>. [June 2011].

44 | SOCIAL ENGINEERING AND PRECAUTIONARY MEASURES THAT DETER RISK

WHAT IS SOCIAL ENGINEERING?

Apart from exploiting holes in your software security systems, crooks find it easier to exploit human nature to gain access to information. This criminal method of s gaining access to your computer is generally known as social engineering, which is a term describing non-technical intrusions relying heavily on human interaction. This often involves inducing people to break normal security procedures.

Humans are helpful by nature, and this is often preyed upon as a weakness by a social engineer to break into computer networks. The social engineer gains the confidence of an authorized user to get him/her to reveal information that he subsequently uses to compromise the security of the network. Most social engineering tricks rely on appeal to greed, appeal to authority, appeal to vanity and/or simple eavesdropping to harvest security information. For example, the social engineer might call an authorized employee to solve some urgent problem requiring immediate network access.

Social engineering is composed of different types of exploits. Some use frauds that often mimic the names of well-known companies to send fake email messages claiming to need your login information or password for so-called security purposes. Others may claim you have won a lottery and they need your bank details to transfer the winnings. Who has not received e-mails claiming that you have won a well-known lottery or a sweepstake? Most often, there is no such lottery or a sweepstake; rather it is an attempt to entice you into participating in fraudulent transactions.

One of the most widely experienced social engineering exploits is scareware or rogue security software. This type of software appears beneficial from the perspective of security, but actually is not. Rather, it generates misleading or erroneous alerts and often induces the authorized user to disclose his/her login information. Such frauds are often found in on-line advertisements, search engine results, social networking sites, e-mails and even in pop-up messages that trick you into thinking that they are a part of your security system.

HOW TO RECOGNIZE FRAUDULENT SOCIAL ENGINEERING SCAMS

- You can familiarize yourself with common telltale signs that social engineering fraudsters use to exploit people. Some of these are:

- Messages intended to create alarm and threats of account closure;

- Offer of money for little or no effort;

- Offer of a deal that is too good to be true;

- Requests for donations to a charitable institute immediately following a disaster that has received publicity;

- Misspellings and bad grammar.

BUILDING UP DEFENSES AGAINST SOCIAL ENGINEERING THREATS

Most organizations do have a level of defense against social engineering threats, but most often this is reactive. After discovering a successful attack, a barrier is erected to make sure the same problem will not recur. However, by the time the solution comes, it is too late and often the repair and remedy is expensive. A more proactive approach preventing such attacks is more effective.

For an effective proactive defense against such a wide variety of social engineering threats, it is necessary to plan your preemptive steps. Broadly, this is to be done in three steps:

- Develop a framework for security management to define a set of security goals for social engineering;

- Undertake risk management assessments;

- Implement defenses against social engineering within your security policy.

It is necessary to define a set of security goals for social engineering and appoint staff members responsible for delivering the goals. A written set of procedures and policies must be drawn up to stipulate how the staff members will handle such attacks from social engineering.

REFERENCES:

1. Rouse, M., Search Security, *Definition Social Engineering*. Available from: <http://searchsecurity.techtarget.com/definition/social-engineering>. [October 2006].

2. Microsoft, Safety & Security Center: *What is social engineering*? Available from: <http://www.microsoft.com/security/resources/socialengineering-whatis.aspx>. [2013].

3. Microsoft, Safety & Security Center: *Email and web scams: How to help protect yourself.* Available from: <http://www.microsoft.com/security/online-privacy/phishing-scams.aspx>. [2013].

4. Microsoft, *How to Protect Insiders from Social Engineering Threats.* Available from: <http://technet.microsoft.com/en-us/library/cc875841.aspx#XSLTsection124121120120>. [2013].

45

THE TDOS EFFECT

WHAT IS TDOS?

TDoS or Telephonic Denial of Service is a rising form of attack and can clog your telephonic lines including your VoIP lines, thereby blocking all incoming calls. Similar to the denial of service attacks, legitimate callers are unable to connect to hospitals, banks, emergency services and many other services over their phone lines.

However, unlike DoS or DDoS attacks, TDoS attacks do not need an army of botnets to initiate the attack. The technology used is simple. Perpetrators clog phone lines simply by calling the number repeatedly in rapid succession. A simple VoIP script calls the number, hangs up, and then redials repeatedly. This overwhelms the victim's line, making it impossible for any incoming call to come through. Moreover, the attackers often use spoofed numbers, which makes it difficult to screen the calls and to differentiate between a genuine call and a TDoS call.

HOW IS TDOS LIKELY TO AFFECT YOU?

Several enterprises require their telephone lines to remain open to receive and respond to emergencies. Fire brigades and ambulance services are examples of such organizations that use the telephonic lines extensively for reaching out to people promptly in emergency cases. If TDoS attacks block their lines, not only will these organizations suffer, many innocent lives are likely to be lost, as people in need will be unable to contact the emergency services in case of fires or accidents.

The main hurdle in differentiating TDoS attacks from a normal call is they appear, and are, perfectly legitimate calls. The only difference is they come from a malicious source and have a malicious intent. It can be very challenging to distinguish such calls, even with hardened VoIP servers using the right protections.

Recent TDoS attacks are part of sophisticated extortion schemes. Attackers first demand payment against an outstanding debt, which is likely to be false. On denial, the perpetrator launches a TDoS attack, inundating the telephonic system or the VoIP system with a continuous stream of calls for unspecified but lengthy periods. The attack prevents both incoming and outgoing calls from being completed.

HOW TO PREVENT TDOS ATTACKS FROM HAPPENING

Enterprises must take adequate steps to secure their VoIP and their telephony systems just as they do for the rest of their network. Since VoIP systems are similar to other computer network systems the enterprise is using, they require the same level of protection against cyber-attacks as any other network server does.

VoIP systems cannot be kept behind legacy firewalls and require application layer gateways or ALG, which are specifically designed to handle VoIP protocols. Such ALGs can prevent SIP directory harvesting, which leads to network level DoS attacks.

For severe TDoS attacks, enterprises may have to contact the FBI or the Department of Homeland Security for further investigation.

REFERENCES:

1. Krebs, B., *DHS Warns of 'TDos' Extortion Attacks on Public Emergency Networks.* Available from: <https://krebson-security.com/2013/04/dhs-warns-of-tdos-extortion-at-tacks-on-public-emergency-networks/>. [1 April 2013].

2. Higgins, K.J., *Hacking the TDoS Attack.* Available from: <http://www.darkreading.com/attacks-breaches/hacking-the-tdos-attack/240155809>. [30 May 2013].

3. Nachreiner, C., Help Net Security, *TDoS: The latest wave of Denial of Service attacks.* Available from: <http://www.net-security.org/article.php?id=1828>. [15 April 2013].

46 | MAINTAINING, MONITORING AND ANALYZING

WHAT HAPPENS WITHOUT LOGGING OF AUDIT RE- CORDS?

Audit logs provide clues that allow administrators to fol- low the trails of attackers within an enterprise's com- promised network system.. Any deficiency in the logging and analysis of the security logs allows the attackers to hide the location of their malicious software and use it to control and monitor activities on the victim's machine.

Even when an attack on the victim's machine is established with certainty, the complete details of the attack and the ex- tent of damage can only be known by studying the complete logging records, provided they have been protected from damage. However, in the absence of solid logs, not only will such attacks go unnoticed for long periods, but also the damage done may well be irreversible.

Attackers using smart technologies can erase their trail effectively. Sometimes the only way to detect such attacks is through analysis of the logging records. Organizations who keep the logs for compliance alone, may not glance at the audit logs, and therefore, may never know when their systems have been comprised, even when the traces of the attack are evident in the unexamined log files.

HOW DOES LACK OF AUDIT LOGS AFFECT THE ORGANIZATION?

With absence of audit logs, an enterprise will be unable to achieve several security-related objectives such as:

- Individual accountability

- Reconstruction of events

- Intrusion detection

- Problem analysis

Audit trails work in tandem with logical access control, as this restricts the use of system resources. This allows monitoring of users suspected of improperly modifying data or introducing errors within a database. The audit trail establishes the "before" and "after" versions of the records. Without the audit trail, it is impossible to establish who made the errors, whether it was the user, the system, the application software or an external attacker.

Audit trails are useful for reconstructing events once a problem has been detected. System logs can pinpoint the exact system activity that led to the cessation of normal operations. For example, with the help of an analysis of the audit trail, it is easy to distinguish between errors induced by operators and errors created by the system.

Logged activities can identify attempts at penetrating a system to gain unauthorized access. However, absence of logging or failure to analyze the existing logs can lead to external attackers gaining access to the network.

HOW CAN THIS THREAT BE MITIGATED?

Use both types of audit records and record them – an event oriented log and keystroke monitoring. Set event based logs to record system events, application events, and user events.

Set the audit trail to include sufficient information, establishing what events occurred and who caused them. For keystroke monitoring, preserve keystrokes along with user identification, as this will enable administrators to determine which specific user entered the keystrokes.

Use at least two synchronized time sources or Network Time Protocol (NTP), and use them on all servers and network equipment. Use the same time stamp for logs as well, so that there is consistency throughout the network.

REFERENCES:

1. The SANS Institute, *Critical Control 14: Maintenance, Monitoring, and Analysis of Audit Logs.* Available from: <http://www.sans.org/critical-security-controls/control.php?id=14>. [2012].

2. NIST Special Publication 800-12, *Introduction to Computer Security: The NIST Handbook.* Available from: <http://csrc.nist.gov/publications/nistbul/itl97-03.txt>. [2012].

3. ThreatTrack Security Inc. Available from: <http://www.threattracksecurity.com/documents/enterprise-security-white-paper-sandboxing-helps-avoid-security-breach.pdf>. [2012].

47 | ARE YOUR WIRELESS DEVICES UNDER CONTROL?

WHAT IS THE THREAT?

Attackers gain illegal wireless access to an organization from outside the physical building. They bypass the security perimeters of the organization using wireless connections to internal access points. Attackers have initiated major thefts of data in this manner.

Wireless devices belonging to traveling officials are often infected by remote exploitation when used in a cyber cafe or during air travel. When reconnected to the network of the parent organization, the exploited devices are then used as back doors to gain access.

HOW DOES IT AFFECT BUSINESS?

Corporate security faces a huge threat from mobile devices, as concluded by a global study on mobility risks. The

Ponemon Institute conducted the study sponsored by Websense in 2012. According to the study covering over 12 countries and 4,600 IT security practitioners, use of unsecured mobile devices led to data losses experienced by 51% of the organizations. More than 30% of the respondents experienced 50% more malware infection from these devices.

There were serious consequences of the data breach. Loss, removal and/or theft of information amounted to 38%, and an additional 38% went for disclosure of confidential or private data.

An attacker may use an unsecured wireless network for clandestine purposes such as spreading pornography. The breached organization, although not privy to such activity, may be drawn into legal wrangles.

Through unsecured wireless networks and devices, attackers can target Internet- banking services that usually send SMS authentication code for each online transaction. That makes it easy for the attacker to raid an account after stealing your login password.

HOW SHOULD RISKS BE MITIGATED?

It is impractical to expect employees not to use their wireless devices in public places such as a cyber cafe. The onus, therefore, is on the organization to mitigate the risks by extending all IT security and acceptable use policies to all mobile devices in the organization.

Rooted devices are easy to use as the user has full privileges to access all apps. However, this is true for the attacker as well, and rooted wireless devices should be refused access to the network.

To protect against data loss, full device encryption may be used along with provision for remote wipe, should a mobile device be stolen or lost. Encryption must be extended to any SD cards in use containing sensitive data.

Automated processes must be established for updating wireless devices so that they reflect the latest security fixes. Manufacturers of wireless devices provide security patches and the devices should be kept up to date.

Employees must be instructed to connect to Wi-Fi networks manually, instead of as peer-to-peer or ad hoc. This usually helps to prevent them from connecting to rogue networks specially designed for stealing information.

Instruct employees to disable file sharing before starting to use Wi-Fi hotspots or other unsecured wireless connections.

Wireless device users must make it a habit to disable the wireless connection on their device when not using them.

REFERENCES:

1. The SANS Institute, *Critical Control 7: Wireless Device Control*. Available from<http://www.sans.org/critical-security-controls/>. [June 2012].

2. Legnitto J., *The Truth about Wi-Fi*. Available from<http://www.privatewifi.com/are-your-employees-compromising-your-company%E2%80%99s-sensitive-information-with-unsecured-mobile-devices/>. [30 March 2012].

3. Prism Risk Assessment LLC. 2012. Available from<https://prismrm.wordpress.com/2012/12/27/unsecured-wireless-networks-can-bring-criminal-investigations-depending-on-who-is-using-it/>. [27 December 2012].

4. Sophos Ltd. Available from<http://www.sophos.com/en-us/medialibrary/PDFs/other/sophossecuritythreatreport2013.pdf> [2013].

48 | YOUR PROCESS OF CONTINUOUS VULNERABILITY ASSESSMENT AND REMEDIATION

Security researchers or vendors discover and report new vulnerabilities in the configuration of devices approved and listed in the asset inventory database. In the absence of any control over detecting these vulnerabilities and subsequent prevention and correction, attackers create exploit code and launch these codes against targets of interest. Dangerous vulnerabilities that are not found and fixed within a significantly short time provide many opportunities for a persistent attacker to break through. The attacker then gains control over the vulnerable machine/s, and has access to the sensitive data contained within.

If there is no process of systematically discovering flaws and subsequently fixing the found vulnerabilities on a proactive basis, the organization faces a significant risk of compromising their computer system and their sensitive data.

However, attackers can exploit the vulnerability scan itself. After having taken control of a machine with local privileges, the attacker waits until the start of an authenticated scan against the machine. As the scanner logs in with the privileges of a domain admin, the attacker may sniff the challenge response to crack it or overtly grab the token of the scanning tool that is logged in. After this, it is a simple affair for the attacker to pivot anywhere and move about in the organization as a domain administrator.

By using a vulnerability scanner that has been validated by SCAP or the Security Content Automation Protocol, automatic scanning may be initiated on a network of systems against common types of flaws such as configuration-based and code-based vulnerabilities. Ideally, the most up-to-date vulnerability-scanning tool must be used daily. The results of the scan must deliver a priority list of the vulnerabilities that are highly critical to all major system administrators, including risk scores comparing the effectiveness of departments and system administrators in reducing risks.

Any vulnerability thus exposed, must be fixed in a timely manner. Critical vulnerabilities should take no more than 48 hours to be remedied. The most common types of threats due to vulnerabilities are listed below:

Threats	Average Occurance
Drive by redirect Payload Exploit site	85.1% 7.5% 2.5%
SEO Fake antivirus	1.1% 0.4%
Others	3.4%

System administrators must correlate vulnerability scans with event logs. This serves two goals. One, the activity produced by the regular scanning tools is logged, and second, attack detection events can be correlated with the earlier reported scan results. This helps to determine if an exploit was used against a known vulnerable target.

It is prudent to dedicate a single account for authentically scanning vulnerability. Do not use the scanning account for any other purpose and tie it to specific machines with specified IP addresses. Allow only authorized employees to access the user interface for the vulnerability management.

In addition to PCs, the growing use of mobile systems and Cloud adoption is opening a new world for exploiters to enter through additional security flaws. Increasing numbers of firms are now talking security practicalities and setting deployment timetables to tackle the menace of vulnerabilities.

REFERENCES:

1. Schwartz, M. J., *7 Top Information Security Trends For 2013*. Available from: <http://www.informationweek.com/security/application-security/7-top-information-security-trends-for-20/240145336>. [27 December 2012]

2. Sophos Ltd. Available from: <http://www.sophos.com/en-us/medialibrary/PDFs/other/sophossecuri-tythreatreport2013.pdf>. [2013]

3. The SANS Institute, *Critical Control 4: Continuous Vulnerability Assessment and Remediation*. Available from: <http://www.sans.org/critical-security-controls/control.php?id=4>. [June 2012].

49

MAINTAINING AN INVENTORY OF ALL AUTHORIZED AND UNAUTHORIZED DEVICES

Meta Description: Any system, including test systems connected to the network for even a short period, may become a relay point for causing damage to an organization.

NATURE OF THE VULNERABILITY

Several rogue nation-states and groups today employ systems to continuously scan the address spaces of organizations they target. They wait and attack any new and unprotected systems that are attached to the network, including test systems. Anything such as a laptop or a PDA, not up to date with patches could be their target. It is easy for any attacker anywhere in the world to find and exploit such systems via the Internet.

Once the attackers have gained internal access, they could quickly find and compromise other such improperly secured computer systems on the network. The local nighttime window is most favored by the attackers to install backdoors into systems before they are hardened the next day.

With advancement of new technology, organizations allow employees to Bring Your Own Devices or BYOD to workplaces, where they are connected to the network of the organization. Many of these devices may already be compromised, and they can be used as a relay point to inflict damage to the organization.

EFFECT ON THE ORGANIZATION

If compromised and exploited, such vulnerability could result in:

- Unauthorized disclosure of data
- Sensitive data, relating to purchase, accounts, inventory, Intellectual Property, resources, marketing and sales may be revealed.
- Unauthorized modification to the system, its data, or both
- Denial of service, access to data, or both to authorized users

Attackers may permanently lock an exploited system to its compromised state, thereby assuring a permanent entry point into the organization every time the system is used. Without a proper inventory control of the hardware and software devices used on the network, an organization will have no way of knowing the entry point of the attackers.

Similar to locking up an exploited system, attackers may disallow authorized users from accessing service and data.

Passwords may be changed and an authorized user may find he is unable to login into his bank account or a CEO unable to access the latest sales projections for the upcoming AGM.

HOW TO MITIGATE THE THREAT

Set up operational rules to make sure users in the organization are running only approved and licensed software on their machines. This has an additional benefit of tracking both under-utilized and over-deployed software licenses, since both issues are financially important to the organization.

Use appropriate software to provide constant automation for asset inventory discovery that will provide New MAC and New Host found alerts, whenever a new device is plugged into the network. Encouraging the use of a standard naming convention for all hosts on the network makes it easy to detect the unauthorized one standing out.

Separate virtual local area networks or VLANs may be created for untrusted devices such as BYOD systems.

Use automated tools to notify security about an unauthorized asset plugged into the network, within two minutes; achieve isolation within five minutes.

REFERENCES:

1. The SANS Institute, *Critical Control 10: Secure Configurations for Network Devices such as Firewalls, Routers, and Switches*. Available from: <http://www.sans.org/critical-security-controls/control.php?id=1>. [2013].

2. BMC Software, *Discover and dynamically track your IT hardware and software assets*. Available from: <http://www.numarasoftware.com/footprints/inventory-management/>. [2013].

3. Eubanks, R., The SANS Institute, *A Small Business No Budget Implementation of the SANS 20 Security Controls*. Available from: <http://cse.spsu.edu/raustin2/coursefiles/id/SmallBusNoBudgetImplSans20SecControls.pdf>. [10 Aug 2011].

ENDNOTES

1. Acronym for "Completely Automated Public Turing test to tell Computers and Humans Apart"

2. A cookie, also known as a web cookie, browser cookie, and HTTP cookie, is a piece of text stored by a user's web browser.

3. Advanced Encryption Standard

4. JavaScript Object Notation

5. Uniform Resource Identifiers

6. Content Scrambling System

7. Information and Communications Technology

8. Annual Trade Show sponsored by RSA Data Security, Inc.

www.ingramcontent.com/pod-product-compliance
Lightning Source LLC
Chambersburg PA
CBHW071420050326

40689CB00010B/1913